Getting Back
Financial

The Newly Divorced Woman's Guide To Money Management

By

Tracy Wetzbarger

Table of Contents

Introduction

"Divorce may be an ending, but it's also a new beginning."

This phrase has been in my head since a friend mentioned it during one of my divorces. (Yes, I've been through all of this more than once). It didn't make much sense at the time as I was caught in the throes of extreme emotion and feeling sorry for myself, but now it's the basis for this book. All divorce proceedings involve several loose ends, both financial and emotional, and they both can take a heavy toll on you and your kids as you struggle to understand your new reality and fight for your financial life.

While the emotional aspect is heavy, taking back control of your finances is a big step towards becoming self-reliant again. Getting your finances under control will help you successfully transition into a new life as a single, independent woman and provide you with the peace of mind and security needed for your future.

We can all relate to several problems we (as newly divorced women) face. The most common is the fear and uncertainty around our finances, how much our lives will change as we navigate our kids' day-to-day needs and expenses, and the challenges of our new circumstances. It is particularly challenging for a stay-at-home mom who has invested so much time in her family and is now suddenly finding herself having to figure out the income side of her new life.

Alternatively, if you are working and building a career, raising kiddos, and going through a divorce, becoming solely responsible for your household finances can be overwhelming and take its toll on you emotionally and physically.

Whatever your situation is, I totally understand it. I have gone through the divorce process twice … once at my request and once after being totally and completely blindsided by the news. Both times I was self-employed and working from home, but the businesses were young and new and didn't bring in the income I needed to continue the way of life as I was accustomed. Both times, I had to sell my home and find a new place to live. Both times, I had to sit down with my bank and credit card statements and face the harsh reality of a budget and where I could cut back expenses to make ends meet. So, I get it. I get the anger and fear. I get the sadness, the "Why me?" and the confusion.

This book is a roadmap to help navigate the twists and turns of post-divorce financial life. Whether you are a stay-at-home mom who needs to reenter the workforce, a career woman facing asset division and the need to up your income game, or someone starting from scratch, I've got your back. This book will provide the tools, insights, and encouragement needed to create a stable and prosperous future. Yes, you are going to have to work at it. Yes, you are going to have to face some uncomfortable financial realities. Yes, you will probably have to make some decisions you'd rather you didn't have to make (like asking your parents to co-sign your new lease at age 42 like I did). But, in the end, you will emerge with a stable and prosperous new tomorrow.

This book is about more than just balancing a budget or creating a spreadsheet (although that will be discussed). It comes from years of experiencing my own divorces and the emotional and financial challenges they both brought.

I will guide you to achieve financial independence, identify and prioritize financial goals, manage and budget your debt and expenses, and set up a financial plan for your future. The objective of this book is to serve as a companion on the journey to financial freedom, not just for your present circumstances but also for the exciting times ahead.

So, let's roll up our sleeves and dive in!

With Peace and Love,

Tracy

Chapter 1:

The Emotional Rollercoaster

"I think we should get a divorce."

"I clearly remember the moment I heard those words, and my world stood still as I slowly sat down on the bed. It seemed as if all the sound had been sucked out of the room, my vision narrowed to a pinprick, and I stopped breathing. As the words bounced around in my head, my brain desperately tried to make sense of what he was saying.

- *"What is happening right now?"*
- *"Why are you doing this when I am getting ready to leave the house to meet a friend for coffee?"*
- *"How am I going to live on just my income? Am I going to be able to stay in this house?"*
- *"What did I do to bring this about? Is there someone else?"*
- *"What do I do now?"*

I slowly started breathing again. I could hear the sounds of the room around me, and my vision returned to see him standing in front of me, facing me, at the end of the bed. Over the pounding of my heart, I heard myself ask if there was anyone else. His answer was adamant that there was not. That turned out to be a bigger lie than I could process at the time. I think so many people can relate to this and applaud you for being so vulnerable and sharing

*I will never forget the next words that came out of my mouth, "You are not going to f*** me over in this divorce!"*

A study in 2022 discovered a rise in divorces, up to 14.56 per 1000 married women in the United States. It's not a pretty number (Loo, 2023).

Divorce is a time of profound change in your life; trust me, it is not merely a legal procedure. It's a wild journey, with highs and lows that include shock, worry, and deep sadness interspersed with anger, grief, and dread.

You will practically explode with emotions that sometimes feel at odds with each other and swing wildly from depression and worry to confidence and strength in a matter of minutes. At times, you'll ask yourself, "Why do I feel happy?" while other times, the nagging voice in your head pokes at the beehive of emotions, telling you that nothing is going right.

Regardless of who initiates it, the impact of divorce—emotionally, physically, and financially—can take weeks, months, or even years to resolve. The emotional after-effects of separation and divorce are high, but despite the chaos, there can be surprisingly strong feelings of relief, hope, and perseverance, those "I got this" moments.

These emotions may seem contradictory, but when you remove a thorn from your side, although it hurts, it sets the healing process into motion, filling you with relief because it eventually won't hurt anymore.

This chapter will help you recognize the many facets of divorce. It requires studying and adjusting your mind and emotions. Divorce is an experience in which the hope for a fresh start and the memory of crushed dreams intertwine.

"I stood slowly up from the edge of the bed and said, "I need to go to the barn to feed the horses. When I get back, I expect you not to be here." I got into my car and drove to the barn, the tears I wouldn't

cry in front of him streaming down my face. Sobbing uncontrollably, I dialed my best friend to let them know what just happened."

Shock and Denial

- *"We should get a divorce."*
- *Shock? Check.*

The first feeling checked off the divorce emotional card is often shock. Your safe bubble of a healthy relationship popped just like that, and you no longer know the truth.

- Was your relationship built on a lie? On deception?
- Or is there something that has changed over time?
- If so, what changed?

We have more questions than answers, and every fiber of our being begs to know "Why"? Your partner, love, and pillar are uprooting themselves and walking away, leaving you to face the world alone. The only home you know has changed.

Shock is a sudden disturbance that causes an intense emotion such as surprise or horror, often characterized by confusion and emotional paralysis. With so many emotions at work, you can't blame your mind for being unable to process the feeling of loss. It is often challenging to comprehend what is going on, your mind can't focus, and you feel it is impossible to make any decision because ... well, what if it isn't the RIGHT decision?

How can you be sure you're protecting yourself and your kids from any adverse consequences of your choices? What should you do? This can leave you feeling like you are living in a dream-like state with no direction and sometimes no memory of the event that caused the shock.

Denial, on the other hand, is often said to be the first phase of grief (more on that to come) and is usually a defensive mechanism that helps you avoid the current pain and distress you're going through. It's common to resist the new reality during the initial few days of a divorce. Instead of acknowledging the separation's permanence, you may hope the situation is temporary and reversible.

You may tell yourself that your spouse is just upset and will be home before you know it or that they'll realize how much they love you, calm down, and come home soon. Of course, it's always easier to divert your attention from the problem at hand by denying its existence in the first place. If I don't think about it, it isn't there.

However, this matter isn't as simple as the game, "If I can't see you, you can't see me." We must avoid running from problems even if it seems like the easiest decision. The longer you suppress and prolong the pain, the more it will hurt when you cannot contain those emotions anymore.

By acting on your denial, you are desperate to protect yourself from the truth of your divorce because it is simply too painful to accept at the moment. But denial only numbs the pain. It doesn't banish it, and you will continue to be confronted by the same sorrow and sadness over and over again, turning the grieving process into a long and complex cycle. Your brain holds these memories; unless you face them, it will keep returning to them.

Short-term denial helps give you the time to organize yourself and accept this significant change in your life; however, in all honesty, it's not practical and pushes you multiple paces back. While you are busy refusing to believe your new truth, your soon-to-be ex is moving forward, formalizing the divorce with a head start. They probably have been working on some details long before they let you know their intentions. The longer you stay in denial, the farther ahead they will be in the negotiating game and the more you can lose.

It's a tough pill to swallow, but I know from experience how difficult it is to experience these emotions while facing a world that expects you to pull yourself together and take a stand. You're only human.

"Upon my return from the barn, I was relieved to see his car was gone. I had spent a good 1/2 hour on the phone at the barn with my bestie, wildly swinging from emotion to emotion. Relief seemed good to settle on for a minute or so. I had no desire to see him or talk to him. Even with my dog greeting me at the door with wild abandon, the silence was profound as I crumpled to the floor. "

Understanding Your Emotions

The reality of divorce is complicated for the mind to reconcile, especially with our preconceived notions and expectations about marriage. We all have an image of married life, even as kids: the white dress, the flowers, the walk down the aisle, and the vows. All that "until death do us part" bullshit.

Because of this dissonance, distress and disbelief may be more intense, often leading to the denial we've previously discussed. Divorce isn't a new concept, nor is it a word we haven't heard before, but to think it's happening to us can cause our entire world to collapse at our feet.

Not only might you be grieving the disintegration of your marriage, but you might also be grieving the loss of hopes, shared experiences, and a future once imagined together. You might feel withdrawn from social interaction and the need for isolation (fueled by guilt, shame, and fear of judgment) as you struggle to understand everything.

Anger and fear will most certainly rear their heads in the emotional challenge of your divorce, and depression and grief can bog you down, making every day feel as if you are wading through mud. Only in this case the mud will be in every corner of your house, reminding you of what was once there but will no longer be.

Believe me when I tell you that intertwined with all these emotions will sometimes be a sense of profound relief, unwavering confidence, acceptance, contentment, and even joy.

It's unbelievable, I know, but it is crucial to understand and experience ALL of the emotions accompanying your divorce to come out the other side happy, content, and whole.

"After sobbing on the floor for a while, I felt the tides inside me suddenly shift. I grabbed a glass of wine and climbed the stairs to our bedroom, the same room where, just a couple of hours before, my world had been destroyed with seven words. I entered, stopped, took a sip of wine, and looked around. At that moment, I decided I would NOT sleep in that room as long as there was any trace of him in it."

Truly Experience Your Emotions, aka "Allow Yourself To Feel"

As we've discussed, experiencing denial for a time is extremely normal during and after a divorce. It may help you to come to terms with your new reality. However, continuous denial and dwelling in the past can be harmful. Accepting these emotions may be difficult, but you must do it.

When you are ready—and I mean ready, ready (not just because someone else told you it was time to pull up your big girl panties and "just get over it already," ready—it's time to confront all of those pesky emotions and get a real handle on where you are right now, who you want to be, and how you will get to your future.

1. Engage In Healthy Expressions

Processing emotions through channels of healthy expression, such as journaling or painting, can be helpful. Meditation is also a practical and very healthy way to process all the feelings surrounding your divorce. No matter what way (or ways) you choose to process your emotions, there is only one rule ... DO NOT hold back in any way.

If you're angry, let it out and scribble ruthlessly in your journal. If you're confused, allow all the colors in your painting to swirl together. If you're sad, let the tears flow uncontrolled in your room before starting your meditation with a clearer mind. Do the tear stains wet your paper? Let it stain and make a mess.

After a few minutes of allowing that emotion to BE, I guarantee that you will find yourself swinging to a place that feels a little better than it did yesterday. Let yourself exist and feel. I have had clients share how thankful they were for this exercise because it allowed them to pause and prioritize themselves for the first time in a long time.

2. Normalize Your Emotions

Emotions don't fit into tidy compartments; they ebb and flow, crawl all over each other, and relentlessly intertwine, leaving us breathless and confused, crying with joy or frighteningly confident. It takes work to understand your emotions, but the first step is to realize they are normal—boringly, tediously, tiresomely normal. Everyone experiences them every single moment of every single day. They cannot hurt you; they are normal and simply exist. Would love to more know about how to do this. Such a mental hurdle sometimes. I am going to email you a paper about this something i got from my therapist bc this is harddd.

3. Seek Out Support

I always advocate that you seek professional help during your divorce recovery. Speaking with a life coach or consulting with an expert in mental health can provide a secure, safe environment to talk about feelings and help you with coping mechanisms specific to you and your situation. You'll feel secure in the hands of someone who deals with such situations professionally and knows how to help you. Take the time to find a compassionate coach (preferably one specializing in divorce) or therapist who is empathetic, kind, and fully understands what you're going through.

It is also crucial for your emotional well-being to create a network of friends and family who will provide empathy and helpful support. In this instance, I emphasize the word 'useful,' as your support network shouldn't drag you back into the depths of denial but allow you to process your emotions and story in your own way and in your own time. While a therapist or coach can help you see things from an outsider's point of view, helping you realize things you've never realized before, your friends and family will provide the sympathy and shoulder to cry on that you so desperately need at a time like this.

"Anger surged through my body as I stripped the bed and remade it with the new sheets I had ordered the week before but hadn't actually used. I removed the bedside table with all his stuff in it, filled a box with his items from the bathroom, scrubbed his sink, and moved every last article of clothing and shoes into the spare bedroom, dumping it all on the bed. I even removed wall art that proclaimed our undying love for each other and replaced it with the oil painting of my daughter when she was an infant that he refused to have hanging in the house. I took a razor blade and removed the wall decals over the bed. Lastly, I removed my wedding ring and placed it in my jewelry box.

I mean, if it was over, then it would be completely over."

Navigating Grief and Loss

A marriage ending is a loss, a loss that involves the process of grieving. Not only are you grieving the end of a relationship, but you are also grieving the end of specific dreams and expectations that the two of you envisioned as a couple.

Grief can (and most definitely will) creep into the voids created in your day. When you realize that something familiar has fallen apart, it can be challenging to move past the shadows of the past and accept the uncertainties of the future. However, the ability to comprehend and handle the pain that follows divorce is crucial for both your emotional recovery and your personal growth.

The health of your mind is also responsible for keeping your body healthy. For example, the feelings of rejection, loneliness, and vulnerability during divorce have many women falling into depression. This may lead to isolating yourself or losing your appetite, meaning you will not provide your body with the required nutrition, making you weak and fatigued (Klobučar, 2015). Not sure where this would fit in, but this made me think about just the simplicity of taking a shower, taking a walk, and eating a meal that is nutritious and just being able to do that while so deep in grief is hard but important.

Not only is grief universal (it happens to everyone at some time in their lives), but it is also very personal. It is not neat or linear. It doesn't have an order or follow any timeline or schedule. How you process your grief is unique to you, and you will do it on your own time. You may sometimes cry, become angry, withdraw from your friends and family, or feel empty and lost. I assure you none of these things are unusual or wrong to feel.

According to Elisabeth Kübler-Ross in her book On Death and Dying, there are five stages of grief. I firmly believe that you do not, and will not, progress through them in any specific order. You may bounce between any stage at any given moment of any given day. However, it's best to prepare, so let's take a look.

Denial

We've mentioned denial before, and we'll study it again. Denial is a way to protect yourself from experiencing mental and emotional trauma caused by your divorce. Denying helps lessen the grief of loss during the early stages of the mourning process, like a shock absorber (Lawler, 2017).

You run from your emotions by denying your loss. This could manifest as disbelief, being unwilling to accept that the ship has sailed, or downplaying the severity of the situation … envisioning the divorce as only temporary.

During this stage, your physical, emotional, and financial reality completely shifts. When reflecting on the time you shared with your spouse, you might wonder, "How do I move on without them by my side?" Your future is something you cannot even begin to grasp at this point, and you may be intensely overwhelmed. Denial helps slow down this sense of being overwhelmed and allows your brain to reorganize.

Anger

Oh, boy! Anger can be a doozy of an emotion during and after a divorce. It can present as annoyance, resentment, or even a desire for vengeance. This stage in the grieving process may last a very long time, or it could be one you sail through with hardly a backward glance.

The loss of your marriage may seem unfair and cruel… and those thoughts can manifest exponentially if you have kiddos. How dare your spouse be so selfish when you have kids to look after? Thoughts of injustice, broken promises, or betrayal can all give rise to anger when it comes to a divorce.

During this period, you may feel a strong sense of wrath and resentment toward your former spouse due to infidelity, falsehoods, or dishonesty. Heightened by this betrayal by the person you formerly loved and trusted, it is hard to move on.

The blow may be more severe for stay-at-home moms or women who might have less financial power when faced with the loss of financial security and the challenges that could follow (Klobučar, 2015). The asset division, custody battles, and various legal procedures accompanying divorce are no joke, and they can leave you frustrated and full of rage.

Remember, this is a normal reaction to the emotional and financial suffering that frequently precedes the end of a marriage. Your anger may be directed at your former spouse, the events leading up to the divorce, or even yourself.

Bargaining

It is common to experience extreme desperation while dealing with loss, almost to the point you would do anything to lessen or stop the suffering. During this stage of grief, you try to negotiate for a change in the circumstances by offering to accomplish something in exchange for being freed from your pain.

Bargaining during a divorce might take the form of wanting to make amends, pledging to change, or agreeing to couples counseling. You may start speculating about "what-if" situations.

- *"Would he want to stay if I just lost some weight?"*
- *"What if I were a better cook? Maybe he'll change his mind about leaving me."*
- *"Do I even need my new job? I can do what makes him happy as long as he stays."*

You may also show a desire to behave differently to save the relationship or get back together.

- *"I will make dinner every night as long as he stays with me."*
- *"I will keep the house cleaner so he'll come back."*
- *"I will join a gym and lose weight just like he wanted me to so he can love me more"* ("Understanding," 2023).

In short, you're placing yourself under the blade, blaming yourself, and offering to change yourself for the sake of someone trying to leave you behind.

Depression

Characterized by intense sadness, despair, and a void in your life, depression often accompanies a divorce. It is not uncommon to withdraw from all social interactions and feel as if you spend all your time reflecting deeply on the significant loss of your marriage.

I call this the curl-up-in-a-ball-in-the-shower-and-cry-your-eyes-out stage. This is when you question if you have the strength to go on. This is when it seems as if everyone else in the world has someone to love while your other half is no longer around to be the missing piece to your puzzle. This is when just getting out of bed feels like an impossibility.

Although depression may feel like the inevitable landing spot after the loss of your marriage, it is not a place you want to dwell forever. I recommend speaking with a mental health professional if you feel trapped in depression or are unable to get past this stage of sorrow.

Depression comes with multiple physical symptoms, such as loss of appetite, exhaustion, difficulty sleeping, and random pains in the body; however, depression can get ugly when it leads to physical agitation, which, in turn, can result in dire consequences (Smith, 2023).

If, at ANY time, you have thoughts of harming yourself or others, reach out immediately to the National Suicide Hotline. Call the National Suicide Prevention Lifeline at 1-800-273-TALK (8255) or call or text 988.

Acceptance

Acknowledging and embracing the fact that your divorce is a reality doesn't mean your sadness, anger, or fear has been lifted or is no longer valid, nor does it imply you are over your loss. However, it does indicate you've come to terms with it and know what it means for you at this exact moment. It's the first of your mind telling you you're ready to move forward (Stolzenberg & Law, 2023).

Sadness and regret may still creep in, but denial, rage, and bargaining will be less common. You will probably even feel differently, with thoughts more along the lines of "I made an excellent choice by going with this" or "My life is so much freer without them in my daily interactions."

You may even feel a sense of relief and calmness start to sweep over you. You can focus on the day-to-day again, and confidence in who you are and where you are going fuels you for the future.

"The morning after "The Announcement," I woke up alone in my bed with a feeling of deep sadness. There were no tears, just a heavy weight in my chest as I lay there and replayed the evening's events. My dog lay snuggled up tightly against my side as I gazed around the bedroom that was no longer 'ours' but now 'mine.' I got up and went to the window as the sun appeared over the horizon, and I clearly remember standing there and saying out loud, "The world is still turning, and the sun is still shining. I can make this day whatever I want it to be. I can make my life whatever I want it to be."

Dealing with Anger and Resentment

During divorce, certain discussions or changes may trigger negative emotions toward your ex-spouse and your situation. It is not unheard of to feel strong emotions such as rage and resentment, but don't allow these emotions to control your mind. If you can't avoid them, focus on your breathing and the practice of tensing and relaxing your muscles. This mind-body connection will help you remain centered and level-headed.

One more crucial step for acceptance and dealing with negative emotions related to your divorce is to practice forgiveness. Your ex-partner might have hurt you during your divorce, leaving you with conflicted feelings. You might even blame yourself for the bad decisions you've made. In both cases, try practicing forgiveness. I know it may seem complicated, and it may take a long time—maybe even years—to finally be able to do this, but trying is better than not giving it a go at all (Sutton, 2023).

Finding Hope and Building Resilience

We've covered handling grief and allowing yourself to experience it, but what you really need to learn is how to reclaim your identity. Who were you before you met your spouse? You've changed a lot since then, no doubt. What parts of you are genuinely you? What do you like about yourself?

Jenny Mahlum, an integrative psychotherapist in New York, states: "Transitioning from we/us to I/me—from being part of a couple to being an individual—can be quite disorienting" (Gillihan, 2023).

If a psychotherapist says it's hard, it must be, but nobody said it would be impossible. It may seem strange, but the easiest way to complete this transition is to imagine dating yourself and rediscovering your preferences without passing any judgment.

Your physical health is just as important as your mental health. Get that body moving through exercise or nature walks, or pick up new hobbies that will divert your mind and result in something productive (Raypole, 2022).

God knows there will be times when you want to curse out the person who hurt you and blame them for everything that's happened. But honestly? Doing this will only serve to trap you in a cycle of hate. Forget blame—move on with your life, and surround yourself with people who love you. Spend time with your family and kids to show them how much you love and need them, just as they need you, and make new friends—you can never have enough.

Embracing Your New Beginning

We've established that life after divorce can be rough but also an exciting opportunity for new beginnings. There's a certain thrill to retaking control of your life. You get to decorate your house the way you want, have the time to try on a new wardrobe or hobby, or go back to school; YOU get to decide.

In the wake of a divorce, you might not be thinking about the chance for a fresh start and new beginnings, particularly if you're having a hard time just getting through the day-to-day stuff. Starting anew entails uncertainty and change but also an opportunity for development, education, and exploring new ideas and avenues.

Approach this golden opportunity to make your life exactly what you want it to be with an open mind and the willingness to adjust to any changes that might arise, be it a new job, a new house, or even a new state (or country). Could be a chance to really talk about the new beginnings, more and new possibilities and a little more here after talking so much about the 5 steps and depressing stuff.. :/ I love the idea of making my life what i want and could read more about that

Wrapping Up

The crazy journey following a divorce is never a linear path. You will veer wildly from left to right and up and down through the highs and lows of your journey. This can feel overwhelming, and you may carry a load of worry and anxiety as you forge your new path.

Try to make a concentrated effort to let go of worry or anxiety (again, I highly recommend a meditation or prayer routine) so you can make decisions with a clear mind. Accept the new beginning as just that: a fresh start to the life you want. And deserve

In this chapter, we explored the ups and downs of a wide range of emotions, such as fear, rage, and sadness, realizing that these feelings are not obstacles but checkpoints on the path to emotional recovery from your divorce.

In the early stages of a divorce, it can be challenging to maintain your composure and carry on with your daily activities as if nothing has happened. It is difficult to care for your house, raise your children, and perform a regular job with your emotional pain along for the ride. At first, you might be shocked or at a loss for words. You may find yourself barely believing this is happening. Soon, your brain kicks into denial to protect your fragile emotions. This may be followed by anger, bargaining, depression, and eventually acceptance. Remember that nothing is ever linear when healing from a trauma. Healing is an ongoing process.

Exercises and Reflections

To process your emotions, you must experience self-reflection and assess your thoughts, what you've done, what you wish to do, and how things have changed around you.

1. Reflect on the decision to divorce

Consider how you feel and what changed or will change around you during and after this process. How do you feel? Why do you feel that way? Is it wrong to feel that way? Why do you think so, and do others agree with you?

2. Visualize the Future

Take time out of your day to meditate and think about your future after the divorce. This can be a few weeks, months, or even years down the line. Seeing and imagining you're getting used to the change and accepting your new life may make it easier for you to cope.

3. Control the Anger

When negotiating, try not to let your anger get the best of you and push you into making hasty decisions. Show control by recognizing how your body reacts to anger and step away for a breather. Postpone the conversation for another time if it gets to be too much, but *never* let the situation get out of your hands.

4. Engage in Self-Care

Don't leave yourself out of the equation. Take some time to do your favorite hobbies or listen to your favorite songs without giving it a second thought. Enjoy yourself as you do your favorite activities, and even invite a bestie to join in (Sutton, 2023).

"Telling my friends and family about what had happened was one of the most excruciating things I have ever done. I felt such a sense of failure and defeat, especially since this wasn't my first divorce. What is wrong with me? Why can't I keep a relationship? Why am I such a

failure in marriage? Why doesn't he love me anymore? What is happening? How will I rebuild my life?

As the days progressed, the questions changed. Who will get all the things? What do I do to get through the day? Where will I get the money to pay the rent/mortgage? Why can't I sleep? How am I going to afford anything? When will this all be over?

*Once I realized my divorce was simply a moment in time, a blip on my life timeline, I was able to get my act together and start to prepare for the real battle ahead ... the negotiations over the things, the money, and the house. I was relieved there were no kids as a result of this marriage, but as he had been an integral part of my children's lives for almost ten years, I knew I needed to be strong as they also processed through this upheaval in their lives. So I squared my shoulders, pulled up my proverbial big girl panties, and marched into my reality with determination and fortitude. After all, I had told him that first night, "You are not going to f*** me in this divorce."*

And I meant it."

I love the prompts and chance to get some emotions out, i LOVE the idea of it being "interactive" i think that also allows for the possibility for it to visually be really beautiful book as well.

Chapter 2:

Assessing and Understanding Your Financial Situation Post-Divorce

"Even though I was the one who asked for the divorce from my first marriage, the denial phase in my second divorce was considerably shorter. We attempted counseling with my second divorce, but when he failed to show up for his first solo appointment, I knew there was no denying what was happening and that I needed to get out in front of everything as quickly as possible. To be ready to take control of my post-divorce financial life, I needed to take stock of everything we owned and everything we owed."

All right, let's get into the nitty-gritty details of post-divorce life.

After a divorce, starting over requires a solid understanding of your financial situation. It is crucial to take control of your finances early in the process, and acquiring a clear understanding of your current financial situation is the most important step towards regaining financial stability and creating an effective plan for a sustainable financial future for yourself and your children.

First step: Know your financial situation! To find a way forward in your new life, you need a proper understanding of your entire financial portfolio, including assets and liabilities (as well as income and expenses). To get your finances under control, you need to know exactly where you stand right now.

The worst thing you can do to yourself is not be in the financial know. Even if your past relationship required your spouse to take care of that aspect, it's irresponsible to remain unaware after your divorce.

If you need help tackling the financial aspects of your newly divorced life, this chapter will provide a list of the documents you need to keep track of to establish yourself financially. When we go through something as emotionally invested as divorce, stability in life can often become a ticking time bomb, but this is not the time for that; instead, this is the time to take control of your economic future. Your goal is to avoid finding yourself in a fragile situation.

Gathering Financial Documents

"What sort of documents do I need?"

Even the most civil of divorces may be unpleasant and chaotic. In addition to being emotionally and psychologically tasking, the mountain of paperwork you must go through can be challenging and emotionally exhausting. However, just because your divorce is final doesn't mean you no longer need that mountain of paperwork. You can find all the information you need to maneuver your post-divorce finances in that mountain ... so embrace the mountain.

Following is a brief list of documents you need in order to understand where you stand financially post-divorce. Please note that every marriage is different, and every divorce is different. There may be things on the list that don't pertain to you, and there may be things that pertain to you that aren't on the list. My general rule of thumb at this juncture in your life is if you think it might be important ... find it and keep it.

1. Personal Documents

Not only will these documents be vital as we set up your financial details, but knowing where they are and having easy access to them at any given time is crucial. This might be the time to go out and get a simple wall or floor safe to keep all your important papers safe and tidy. It doesn't have to be large or pricey; I found mine at Costco (or Sam's Club) many moons ago. It just needs to be large enough to hold your documentation and one you can secure to the wall or floor.

Important personal documents you want to keep close by include birth certificates (for you and your kiddos), social security information for all of you, citizenship papers, any legal name change documentation, and, of course, your finalized divorce papers (I recommend having multiple copies of your divorce papers on hand and within reach).

Also, ensure you have easy access to medical records, health insurance, life insurance policies, records of judgments, collections, and any bankruptcy filings. Be sure to also round up immunization records for your kiddos, passports, real estate documents, asset valuations (such as jewelry or antique appraisals), vehicle titles, and any documents pertaining to a trust and/or will.

2. General Financial Documents

You can only plan for the future by knowing what's in your pocket. These documents help you determine the distribution of assets post-divorce and understand what falls under your name when planning for the future.

- **Divorce decree** with details of the terms of divorce, such as child support, property and asset division, and child custody. These documents prove to be helpful in financial matters post-divorce.
- **Income documentation** This includes any form of income, such as pay stubs, lease agreements for any rental properties you may own, K-1 and W-2 forms, and 1099s. Your divorce papers may again fall into this category if you receive maintenance or child support payments. If your monthly income fluctuates in any category (self-employment is a

perfect example of fluctuating monthly income), I recommend putting an average on your list. It will help you stay within the budget we will be building in upcoming chapters.

- **Employment records** with the details of any added benefits such as health insurance, life insurance, retirement, and the like.
- **Banking information** from ALL your banks (If you do not have a bank account in your name only ... run, do not walk to the bank, and DO IT RIGHT NOW!). It would help to have monthly bank statements documenting bank charge notices, account balances, transactions, and joint debts or loans.
- **Brokerage statements and certification of** mutual funds, stocks & bonds, etc.
- **Retirement account statements** and pensions, including 401(k)s, IRAs, and other investment accounts.
- **Wills and trust agreements.**
- **Insurance policies** such as life insurance with updated beneficiaries (you DO NOT want your ex-spouse as a beneficiary unless it is in your divorce papers), health insurance, vehicle insurance, property insurance, and so on.
- **An inventory of any safety deposit boxes** to secure related documents and valuable assets. Please take pictures of all the contents for your records.
- **Business documents and financial statements** such as Profit and Loss statements and Balance Sheets used to assess business assets and income for any business you own or are a partner in (Bond, 2023).
- **Tax returns** for at least two years to determine income, assets, deductions, and liabilities (includes all business returns).
- **Current value of any property** you own.
- **Any trusts or documents of inheritance** to give you a holistic view of possible wealth resources should the situation call for it ("Financial Documents" n.d.).

- **Child support and maintenance orders** detailing support payments, their duration, and reference to any modifications.
- **Debt documents.** Arguably, getting your debt documents in order isn't nearly as much fun as seeing all the stuff you own, but seeing how much you OWE is just as critical to your financial health. During your divorce, the debts of the marriage are divided up, as well as the assets. This is where you want to round up all those pesky loan documents, such as car payments, mortgages, personal loans, student loans, credit cards, tax debt, property liens, lawsuits, etc., for the portion of debts that were assigned to you during your divorce. You can also check your credit reports for any debts (Bond, 2023).
- ***Child Care Documents.*** Lastly, you'll need to see what portion of your wealth contributes to the well-being of your kids and their education. Make sure to save the documents marking the details of child custody and child support, and keep a list of any big decisions you've planned for your kids, such as higher education. You can never make independent decisions without considering your children; it's part of being a parent and a vital responsibility ("Child Custody," n.d.).

3. Assets and Liabilities

After settling the legal difficulties of your divorce, making a detailed inventory of your assets and obligations is one of the first and most important steps toward financial freedom. It is likely a complete value assessment of what you both owned and owed during your marriage was completed during your divorce (this is part of the mountain of documents we mentioned earlier), as well as a list of what each of you got during the divorce with their current values. It's time to dig out that divorce decree and deep dive into listing the assets and liabilities assigned to you.

- **Real Estate Assets**

We will proceed with this part of the conversation under the premise that the division of any real estate assets in the divorce has been completed and that deeds and mortgages have been set up in your name only. If you need help, talk to your real estate agent, financial planner, and attorney to ensure you do this correctly and as soon as possible.

Locate any deeds, mortgage papers (including recent refinancing), quit claim deeds, appraisals, and tax assessments on any properties assigned to you in your divorce. List out the value of each property as well as any loan balances and monthly payments. After identifying the property you have on hand, it is time to assess its worth by researching its market value, equity, and possible mortgage and tax applications while also considering the benefits you'll get from selling these assets ("Denver Marital," 2018).

The difference between the value of the property and the outstanding mortgage is the equity or net value of the property. That is the amount you can put in your pocket if you decide to sell (less any selling costs and fees). For example, your house appraises at $400,000, and your outstanding mortgage is $360,000. Your equity in the home is $40,000. Be sure to list the equity of each property on your asset list.

- **Liquid Assets**

Liquid assets refer to any bank accounts (savings or checking) in your name and any cash you have stashed in your safe or safety deposit box.

List the accounts by bank name, account number, and each account amount as of a specific date.

- **Vehicle Assets**

This category includes not only your car but also any boats, RVs, motorcycles, etc., you received in the divorce. Many vehicle value estimators can be found online with a simple Google search. Once you have the value of your vehicle assets, list them along with any remaining loans and monthly payments.

Just like real estate property, the difference between the vehicle's value and what you owe is the equity or net worth.

For example, Your car shows an online value of $25,000, and you still owe $10,000. The net value of the vehicle is $15,000. You would receive that amount if you sold it for total value and paid off the remaining loan. Be sure to note the equity value of each vehicle on your asset sheet.

- **Retirement Investments**

Again, for this conversation, we will assume that all the legal parts of the retirement account asset division and assignment paperwork from the divorce have been completed, and the relevant accounts are listed in your name only. If you still need to do this, make sure your attorney has explained the ins and outs of your particular situation and that you completely understand the ramifications.

Retirement investments may include employer-sponsored plans that guarantee a certain payout upon retirement (usually based on years of service and income), 401 (k) plans, IRAs, annuities, etc.

Next, assess statements related to these pension and retirement accounts. Gauge the impact of tax on withdrawals, transfers, and penalties to gain insight into your investments ("Assessing the Assets," 2023).

Once again, list each account, account numbers, and values as of a particular date.

- **Non-Retirement Investments**

Non-retirement investments can come in various forms, and many can present unique issues with division during a divorce. For this part of the conversation, we will assume again that all the legal paperwork and dance moves have been completed and that you have sole ownership of the investment as ordered by the Court.

The most common non-retirement investments are traditional investment accounts such as mutual funds, stock and bond accounts, and accounts opened through a brokerage account like E* TRADE or TD Ameritrade or a financial planner.

However, you may also have acquired assets that are not publicly traded and are often subject to external forces like monetary policy, political instability, or extreme weather. If you own accounts in this category, I recommend interviewing financial planners to ensure these investments suit you.

- **Life Insurance Policies**

Whole life insurance may have a "cash value" that the policyholder may remove as part of a divorce settlement division of assets. Term life, on the other hand, is not regarded as an asset as it has no value except for when the insured dies. This is an excellent time to remind you to make any beneficiary changes to your life insurance policies.

- **Business Ownership**

Once again, we will assume all the legal moves to divide or transfer ownership of a business have been completed. If business ownership is part of your asset assignment from the divorce, you must understand your financial role in this assignment. I recommend retaining an attorney's services to ensure you understand the complexities of owning (and possibly running) this business. Things to know include whether or not you are a key contributor to the company either via your time or money (as an owner/employee or investor), what legal liabilities you may have, and the ramifications and benefits of selling your share of the business if you should so desire.

Look into the latest statements of every investment, whether stocks, properties, or others. Assess the capital gain and potential growth profit if you sell these investments. Remember that taxes ruin dreams, so watch out for these cuts and asses the total profit you'll gain from your assessments ("Assessing the Assets," 2023).

4. Liabilities and Expenses

Now that we've identified your assets and income, all the things you "own," it's time to put all those debt documents you rounded up earlier into your list so you can see all the things you "owe."

Granted, this is not as fun and may bring about considerable anxiety and maybe even some depression as you get a good look at where you stand financially.

However, without knowing where you are currently with your finances, we cannot plan for your future finances. In other words, you must have a starting point on your map in order to reach your destination, or you are just driving around with no direction.

Although liabilities and expenses sound similar (and they are close cousins as they are both obligations you must pay), they are actually two different animals. Liabilities are something you owe set over a specific time period. Some examples of liabilities include mortgages, car loans, student loans, personal loans, credit card balances, etc. I advise you to pay off your debts and liabilities as soon as possible to avoid becoming a victim of high interest rates (Hayes, 2024).

On the other hand, expenses are daily, weekly, or monthly costs of living. Some examples are rent, utilities, phone, groceries, gas, bus passes, entertainment, eating out, clothing, school activities, insurance, pet costs, etc. Basically, look through your checking account or credit card statement to make a list of everything you spend money on in a month. Put all of this on your list under expenses and an average of what you pay monthly for each expense.

5. Don't Forget Spousal and Child Support

In the most basic of terms, spousal and child support are payments made by one former spouse to the other as a result of the divorce. However, there is a great difference between them.

- ***Spousal Support***

Spousal support is provided by one party to the other if they have no or considerably less income compared to a comparative marriage lifestyle. So, if your ex has a higher income and you fear that you won't be able to support yourself after divorce, you can apply for spousal support in Court. This decision will consider your

- age
- income
- assets and property
- education and career
- living expenses
- new partners (according to relevancy).

In the same context, if you are the breadwinner, your ex can apply for spousal support from you. The Court settles spousal support. If the circumstances change, such as if the requesting party starts earning a higher income, this matter can be revisited and reviewed.

- ***Child Support***

Child support, on the other hand, refers to funds provided by the non-custodial parent to the custodial parent to support the child and their needs. With children, it's vital to remain firm in your stance. Consider their requirements, such as clothes, education, housing, and so on.

It is, no doubt, a stressful situation, but child support is essential, as it will dictate how your child will lead their life in the first few years after a divorce, or at least until you get back on your feet. Courts also consider the child's lifestyle, and if the child has special needs, the support payment will be settled to fulfill these needs. A parent's debts and loans may also determine their capacity to support the child.

There are unfortunate circumstances when one party refuses or avoids paying support. In that case, Ta-da!, legal mediators, attorneys, and the court to the rescue. Find that spouse and hold them accountable for running away from their responsibilities. Don't shy away from legal help to set a legally binding framework that ensures you're not cheated from your court-ordered agreement.

To ensure you have fair treatment and rights, look into hiring a family law attorney who'll help advise, support, and represent you when necessary. Avoid unnecessary disputes and complications on your side as much as possible. You and the kids don't need that negativity in your lives when you're heading toward a brighter future ("What's the Difference," n.d.).

Whether you are receiving or paying child or spousal support will dictate whether this is income or expense on your list.

Importance of Understanding Your Financial Status

Okay, take a deep breath and pat yourself on the back because you just finished a very important step in getting your financial life back in control.

As much as this may stress you out, it's essential to do all of this right now so you don't have to stress about it every day in the future because you're unsure of where you stand.

Understanding all of this gives you a comprehensive view of your financial situation and will help guide you through the rest of the chapters of this book on your way to financial independence.

Remember, the more informed you are about your financial status (assets, income, liabilities, and expenses), the more responsible decisions you'll be able to make, and the easier it will be to take back control of your financial future. This information will enable you to make those decisions confidently and create and live an independent life for yourself and your kiddos free of panic, fear, and stress. Stability and security are your goals. Confidence and knowledge of your financial status are your friends.

Determine your net worth.

Using the net worth worksheet found "here" create a comprehensive list of your assets and liabilities.

If your total debt, such as credit cards, mortgages, student loans, car loans, etc., exceeds your total assets, such as your house, liquid assets, retirement accounts, investments, vehicles, etc., you will show a negative net worth.

Is that bad? Well, it's certainly disheartening, but don't feel dejected. Simply take the information into the upcoming chapters, where we will help you shift and refocus your energy on your financial priorities. You will find yourself bouncing back in no time.

Remember that stability and security are your goals, confidence and knowledge are your friends, and relief will come when you live a healthy and peaceful life. Keep your chin up—there's a lot more to learn ahead.

"After negotiating everything in the divorce, I finally got to see not what WE owned and owed, but what I owned and owed. Although I didn't bring a ton of debt to being single this time around (I had to declare bankruptcy after my first divorce and learned a vital lesson about carrying debt), the asset side of things was mediocre at best for my age, and my income and expenses were dismal."

Chapter 3:

Setting Financial Goals: Your Blueprint for the Future

"As I contemplated the numbers before me, I distinctly remember a feeling of despair sinking deep into my bones. How was I going to do this? Suddenly, I had more expenses than income, a new business that was barely off the ground (and certainly not making any money), and I had to move out of my home in a few weeks. As a certified life coach, I knew I would have to dig deep into my bag of tricks to find a way out of my predicament. I also knew it would take dedication and hard work to get where I needed to be. It was glaringly obvious I needed a plan, and I needed one SOON because, with all the things I didn't know, there was one thing I DID know... I wasn't going to move in with my parents!"

As I mentioned, the journey from denial to acceptance is long and tedious. You will second guess yourself at every turn when you're managing your finances alone, and you will need every bit of planning and discipline to guide your success post-divorce, even while you grapple with emotional turmoil.

Taking up such a massive challenge is daunting, and it's normal to be afraid at first:

- *"I've never done this before!"*
- *"How am I going to pay for a place to live?"*

- *"There is no way I can do this all alone."*
- *"How will I ever be able to afford anything?"*
- *"Will I starve?"*

Questions like these will constantly hassle you, dragging you down as you juggle your emotional health and finances. You're running blind, on your own, in a new reality governed by your everyday financial decisions.

I'm here to help you remove the blinders, pull up your big-girl panties, and get financially savvy. It will be challenging. It will get messy. You may spend some time feeling the entire world is out to get you … there is no sense trying to paint it any other way. Still, as you learn to cope, you will find you don't need to depend on anyone else and can do fine on your own. You will not only accept your new reality but grow and thrive with it!

Post-divorce means not only will your household income decrease, but your expenses may increase as you deal with court costs and attorney fees. You may need to pay for child care to work more hours, go to school, or work on your career. Establishing a new place to live, dealing with rent or a mortgage, furnishing your new digs, and getting utilities in your name also require financial planning.

Right after your divorce, you will be overwhelmed with the need to earn money while still navigating the emotional rollercoaster that threatens to cripple you. This chapter will show you how to set goals for yourself - tiny steps guiding you toward financial freedom so you can walk with your head up high, knowing you don't need anyone else but yourself.

In Chapter 2, we set out to gather all your financial information in one place so you can see exactly where you stand right now. You may feel confident about your financial situation now, or you may be trembling in your shoes and feeling your blood pressure climb as you contemplate the future for you and your kiddos.

To get where you want to be, you must know where you are starting. That's why I had you do all the work in the previous chapter. Now, we will start thinking about where we want to end.

Short-Term vs. Long-Term Goals

"Setting goals is the first step in turning the invisible into the visible."-Tony Robbins.

Your reasons for occupying space on this giant blue planet are your dreams. Dreams are big, out-there aspirations. They feel nebulous and complex (if not impossible) to define to someone else. They shift and swirl in your mind and seem hard to pin down.

Goals, on the other hand, are a series of steps toward achieving your dreams. They are often moving targets that require dedication and focus to achieve. They are specific, down-and-dirty details that can help you achieve your dreams.

Once you start writing out your goals and making plans, life will seem less frightening because you'll have a roadmap as a guide to remind you of your next steps. This way, instead of feeling lost and shooting blindly, you'll feel much more confident and composed as you embark on this process of self-discovery and independence.

Bill Copeland states, "The trouble with not having a goal is that you can spend your life running up and down the field and never score." Right after the divorce, you will be overwhelmed with the need to earn on top of the emotional rollercoaster that seems to cripple you. The silver lining, however, is that setting financial goals will motivate you to get back on your feet and find just how strong you can be. Financial independence is a liberating, unfettering journey that you will embark on, and you're not alone, either. Over half of American women ages 25 and older say they do not consider themselves financially secure, and 77% of low-income women say the same ("Half of American Women," 2023). This chapter will show you how to set small goals for yourself - tiny steps guiding you toward your freedom so you can walk with your head up high, knowing that you don't need anyone else. We'll be looking at this in several stages.

First, let's talk about long-term goals. These are set a bit farther out on your timeline. They are markers along the road to your dream. Some examples of long-term financial goals might be owning your home, retiring, traveling, education, investing, or even starting a business.

On the other hand, short-term goals are those more immediate goals that you will focus on daily. They will get you to the long-term goal markers on the way to your dream.

We must identify and define our dreams before we can even begin setting goals. Ask yourself, "What do I want most regarding my finances?" This is your Financial Big Dream. (There are other areas of your life where you will have dreams, but we will stick to financial dreams for this book).

Just as important as having the dream is to know exactly WHY you have that dream. The "why" will help establish your long and short-term goals. The "why" will keep you focused and moving forward every day, even when you are curled up on the shower floor sobbing your eyes out at the injustice of everything that has happened to you.

Let's practice this a bit.

For example, perhaps your Financial Big Dream is "I want to never worry about money again." Now, you are going to ask yourself one simple question three times about the answer to each previous question:

"Why is this (never worrying about money again) important to me?"

"This is important to me so I can make my own financial decisions."

"Why is this (making my own financial decisions) important to me?"

"This is important to me because I no longer want to depend on someone else's whims in my financial decisions."

"Why is this (no longer depending on someone else's whims) important to me?"

"This is important to me because then I don't have to worry about my rent increasing beyond my budget or having to leave my home because my landlord has decided to sell."

Aha! So this is (one of) the current "whys" to your Big Financial Dream of never having to worry about money again ... "I don't want to be homeless."

Now, let's use that "why" to start setting your goals.

If your why is that you don't want to lose your home due to your landlord's whim, then perhaps a long-term goal is to buy your own house. (It's long-term because this won't happen tomorrow or within the next couple of months).

Great! Let's explore this long-term goal a bit more and see how setting a series of shorter-term goals will get you closer to owning your own home and one step closer to your dream of never having to worry about money again.

First, you need to consider the long-term goal you're setting out to achieve and the steps you will need to take to achieve it. Let's use our example of buying your own house and start by asking yourself:

- *"What must I do immediately to buy my own house?"*
  - *Example Answer: save money for the downpayment*
- *"Where do I start in saving money?"*
  - *Example Answer: Write down a budget to see where I can start saving money."*
- *"What's the next step?"*
  - *Example Answer: Earn enough money to make a mortgage payment on my own."*

Once you have reasonable answers to these questions, make them your short-term goals and work toward them monthly, weekly, and daily. This will prevent you from being overwhelmed by the long-term goal you want to achieve.

Completing your short-term goals adds up to achieving your long-term goals. For example, to reach your long-term goal of owning your own home, you'll need smaller goals, like saving enough money to cover your down payment, earning enough to make the mortgage payment on your own, creating an emergency fund for unexpected expenses, and so on. It is necessary to balance both types of goals because the long-term goal will keep you going as you achieve the short-term, and the smaller goals make the larger ones seem achievable and realistic.

Winston Churchill once said, "Success is not final; failure is not fatal: it is the courage to continue that counts" (n.d.) Success is an ongoing journey, taking one little goal at a time as you work toward a larger goal.

Setting SMART Goals

It's EASY to say you have goals. It's HARD to actually accomplish them. How often do we say we will lose weight, but it never seems to happen? (Or is that just me)?

Often, we STATE goals, but we don't actually SET them. Setting goals requires dedication and focus to accomplish them in a particular time. This is also known as setting SMART goals. I can explain:

1. Your goal must be **Specific**. Always consider the vocabulary (the words used) in your goal. Never state a goal as "I need to" or "I want to." Instead, always state it as "I will".

Let's use one of our short-term goals for home ownership ... saving the downpayment.

By being specific, you define a solid goal you can work toward.

For example, "I will save money for a downpayment on a new home."

See how that goal is specific? You didn't say, "I will save money." That statement has no meaning and is not tied to a long-term goal. That is STATING a goal, not SETTING a goal.

2. Your goal needs to be **Measurable**. Think of quantities at this juncture, as this will make your goal even more 'real' in your mind. Ask yourself how much you will need to achieve your goal or how much you need to do to achieve it. Give it a number. This is how you will know when you are done with the goal.

Let's use our same example of saving money for a downpayment on a new home. Your goal may say, "I will save $30,000 for a downpayment on a new $300,000 home."

See how measurable that is? Now you know exactly how much you will save, and you can devise a plan to save that amount.

3. Make it **Attainable**. You've decided what you want to achieve, right? But is it even possible? More importantly, is it reasonable? If you aim too high, you might get frustrated along the way. If your short-term goal of saving $30,000 isn't sensible for you right now because you don't have a job, the $30,000 needs to be another long-term goal while your new short-term goal is to nail down that paycheck increase.
4. Keep it **Relevant**. Make sure the short-term goal aligns with your broader, long-term goal. If you're aiming for a business in baking, learning to weave baskets might not be relevant to your goal. In our example, your goal of saving $30,000 for a downpayment is undoubtedly relevant to your long-term goal of purchasing your home.
5. Make sure your goal is **Time-Bound**. Set reasonable deadlines to motivate yourself to complete a goal. If you set a wonderfully specific, measurable, doable, pertinent goal

but don't set a deadline, you might spend the next year trying to complete one step of the process because you don't have a deadline to speed things up!

Add one last clause to your short-term goal: "I will save $30,000 for a downpayment on a new $300,000 home by my 40th birthday. (You can also set a specific calendar date for your goal, for example, 'by December 31, 2026'). Ensure your deadline is reasonable, as too many missed deadlines might only demotivate you and keep you from completing your goal.

Now, set your own SMART financial goal(s), ensuring your objective has all five qualities. All of your goals need to be SMART, both long-term and short-term.

It's not uncommon for you to need to break your short-term goals down into even shorter-term goals. For example, if your goal of saving $30,000 is longer than a couple of months, break it down into smaller SMART chunks. One might be, "I will make an extra $1000 for my downpayment savings by the last day of this month by selling my special recipe spaghetti sauce." Specific, Measurable, Attainable, Relevant, and Time-bound.

One more critical thing: Write your SMART goals down and post them somewhere you will see them daily. Without this 'in-your-face' tactic, it's easy to get caught up in all the day-to-day activities and not work on your goals.

Work through the short-term goals and focus on the long-term ones. Do whatever it takes to keep you moving away from your trauma and toward your dream.

Yoga instructor Adriene Mishler said, "Remember, the hardest part is showing up, but you can do it" (2021).

Setting Specific Financial Goals

As I mentioned earlier, financial goals should be concrete. You cannot simply proclaim that you want to be financially stable and out of debt by the end of this year.

Instead, set specific, reasonable goals based on the SMART goal-setting method. Remember the importance of setting numbers and dates for your financial liberation.

Since you now also know how to take account of your finances, use what you know to create your goals. For example, if you are in debt and can pay off an additional amount every month based on your current pay scale, perhaps your goal could be: *"I will pay off an additional $1000 of my debt per month starting next month."*

Balancing your goals and their attainability and timeliness can be an ordeal. Often, it is only through trial and error that you hit that sweet spot. If you miss deadlines, I'd much rather you rewrite the goal than trash it altogether. If it happens repeatedly, then that goal might not be realistic for you, and you need to come up with a different one, such as "I will pay off an additional $500 of my debt per month starting next month".

Here are some tips that may help when you're trying to stay attainable and timely with your goals:

1. Determine how much time a task will take and prepare your calendar accordingly.
2. Organize yourself and your workflow. I often break my monthly short-term goals down into weekly ones. For example, you can break that monthly $1000 paydown of debts into, "I will put $250 into my savings account every Friday to use as an additional $1000 debt payment at the end of each month. (The bonus is that the money isn't in your checking account, where you can accidentally spend it on wine and new shoes!)
3. Remove non-essential tasks. Remember, everything has to be relevant to your goal. For example, don't add to your to-do

list to sign up for an underwater basket weaving class when saving money.

4. Finally, plan for the next goal and make a to-do list. Making a to-do list and checking off tasks from it will keep you motivated and ready to face the next task(s) ("Time Management," n.d.).

Setting Saving, Spending, and Earning Goals

When you embark on a journey alone for the first time, it can be a massive, almost brutal jump. You will have to adapt to it, and the sooner the better. Shared finances supported your former lifestyle, but now you must manage that alone. There are three main factors you need to consider here.

The first consideration is **earnings**. Being new to the financial world, this will likely be your primary worry. Earning is essential to things like putting food on the table and keeping a roof over your head. Your first set of goals should focus on how much you need to earn to meet everyday expenses, which we will discuss in an upcoming chapter.

While you try to earn—and this can take some time as you're still learning—you can also work on your **spending** goals. Although you might be used to a lifestyle where somebody shared your expenses, now you have to cut down on costs to make the most of your earnings. Remember that a penny saved is a penny earned.

Now that you've balanced how much you can reasonably earn and how you can cut down on your expenses—and trust me: you need to plan quite a lot to figure out just how much you can do without—you need to try to set aside some money for **savings**.

It may feel overwhelming to save money, especially when living paycheck to paycheck. However, you need to push yourself and squeeze in a few short-term goals to save a tiny bit wherever possible. These savings can become your emergency fund for setbacks, allow you to take a break, or cover some inevitable loss.

Knowing you have some money to cover unexpected but necessary expenses can act as a motivator to grow your savings. Moreover, if you invest small amounts from the beginning, you can add to your earnings without working for them. Trust me: passive income, the kind that comes automatically, can be an enormous relief. No matter how difficult—ludicrous, even—saving might seem, you MUST figure out a way ... even if it's just $5/week.

Let's return to your goals. Do they fall into any of these categories? All three categories are pivotal for attaining your long-term goals, and you must have a healthy balance between them. Trying to earn enough without letting go of your former lifestyle is unrealistic when you're the sole breadwinner. Trying to squeeze out everything you need by cutting costs could make your lifestyle uncomfortable. In both cases, you will likely be unable to set anything aside for savings, which is another dangerous position. All three considerations require sacrifices, but if you balance them efficiently, you'll be well on your way.

Importance of Rewarding Attaining Goals

Setting goals is the first step in your process. Working to achieve them is another story. As we've seen, post-divorce life is an adventure where you'll navigate or learn to navigate all-new territory. You're in the process of getting over the trauma, but it's still in progress. Given your emotional state, you need to find reasons to celebrate, motivate yourself, and remind yourself that you're becoming a more robust version of yourself. One way to do this is to reward yourself when you achieve a short-term goal.

There's a science to rewards, too. When you anticipate something unique about to happen, your body gets a surge of dopamine, making you feel happy about your work. A happy person will likely be more productive while trying to achieve something. By celebrating the small stuff, you're giving your body and mind solid evidence that your effort was worth it ("Achieving Your Goals," 2018).

As we just saw, the advantage of short-term goals is that they have tiny steps to cover, which allows you to achieve your final goal systematically. Each step is a milestone that marks how you're growing, and each one is worth celebrating because your growth matters to you. Prove to yourself that you matter and that your growth matters, too.

Now, let's talk about your psychological self and rewards. Your subconscious is a mighty thing. When you reward yourself for achieving a goal, it shows your subconscious that you are growing. You feel good about yourself and believe you will get where you want to be.

As Dr. Joseph Murphy says in The Power of Your Subconscious Mind, "Whatever you impress upon your subconscious mind, the latter will move heaven and earth to bring it to pass. You must, therefore, impress it with right [sic] ideas and constructive thoughts" (Murphy, 1963, p. 47).

If the mental picture you create is that of a road to success, that is what your subconscious will strive towards. Therefore, rewarding yourself is one way to communicate with your subconscious and facilitate a desirable outcome, motivating yourself to complete the next task.

Let's look at some things you might do for yourself. The rewards don't have to be expensive (or cost anything at all); they just have to be from you for you.

- Read a new book (It can be online if the budget's tight).
- Take an at-home spa day.
- Make (or buy) yourself some divine dessert.
- Take time for a game night with friends.
- Clear out your schedule for a movie, a walk, a new hobby (like painting or knitting), or anything you like.

You know yourself best!

Developing a Financial Plan

So far, we've discussed your current financial status and how to set goals. Now, we will create a financial plan, one step at a time, by designing and laying out your SMART goals. Your goals form little steps toward your larger financial plan. You'll feel much more confident once you have a written idea of what you're going to do, and this confidence will keep you moving forward when you're going through a rough patch.

Put your goals in order and see if everything balances out. This will give you a roadmap from the beginning to the end, connecting the dots to your long-term goal.

For example, your long-term goal of home ownership may include other goals besides just saving for the down payment. You may need to raise your credit score to qualify for a mortgage by yourself. You may need to pay off your debts before you can raise your credit score. You may need to get a job before you can pay off the debts. Write each of these needs as SMART short-term (and maybe even break them down into shorter-term) goals and post them where you will see them daily.

You're setting a timeline to achieve your long-term desire so it's a well-planned, achievable goal. You're also setting priorities. It may be unreasonable to plan to set aside all your spare money for the down payment on your new home when you're drowning in debt and collecting interest. Still, at the same time, you also need to see movement toward your dream of home ownership to keep that long-term goal alive and well.

Your financial plan needs to include enough money to cover your monthly budget (we will discuss establishing your budget in a future chapter) and enough for your short and long-term goals for debt repayment, investments, a retirement fund, and home ownership. Decide what you need to prioritize and allot a portion of your earnings to each.

Remember, divorce takes an emotional toll. You will have highs and lows as you navigate your financial plan. What's important is that you have something to keep you moving forward with taking control of your financial life. Use your financial plan to see how far you've come on the road to your financial independence.

Dealing with Financial Setbacks

After setting out your financial plan, you'll want to put it into action and bring it to life, and that's the spirit we need! However, it will help to remember you are only human. You can control your actions to a great extent, but leave some room for the fact that you have been through a devastating event in your life and are new to dealing with financial matters all on your own.

Things will happen. You might fall sick, or something might break down at the worst possible time. Remember, you're not alone. It happens to everyone. The important thing is to accept the situation and give yourself some space to heal. Trust me, you can pick up the pieces, readjust your goals, and start over if you allow your mind and body some breathing space. Breathe. It'll pass, and you'll be so much stronger and more experienced when it passes.

As you travel along the learning curve of financial independence, you will discover things about yourself: new limits, new strengths, and new talents. Sometimes, you'll need to tweak your short-term and long-term goals to accommodate these new facets of yourself as you discover them. Maybe you're not good at selling your special secret spaghetti sauce on the side because it takes too long to make it when you're working all day. Maybe one of your goals was too intense, leading to burnout. Perhaps you forgot to leave room for some necessary "me time" or natural setbacks in your timeline.

Once you understand this about yourself, you can modify your goals to suit your needs and purposes. Goals are good, but they sometimes work out differently than planned. Sometimes, they suggest a better route, often opening new avenues on your road map when things refuse to go as planned. Cherish these setbacks as each one is another step toward self-discovery. There's no right way and no ideal timeline to follow. Know that you are exactly where you need to be at all times.

Making Goals Visual

Now that you've set your goals, it is time to establish them by making them visual. Let your creativity loose.

You can start with sticky notes or colored paper. Get colored pens, markers, your favorite stationery, or anything you feel will look good all around the house. Get excited about starting on a new goal!

Draw out little reminders on your material of choice: cut out pictures, doodle, sketch ... whatever you'd like. If your goal is to save for a downpayment, draw the house you want. Draw what you think you'll look like when you have fewer debts. What treat will you give yourself? Add pictures and support them with keywords, deadlines, and details. The more heart you pour into this stage, the more you'll be excited about completing that goal.

Finally, put these sticky notes all over the house. Put them in your favorite spots and your least favorite ones. Do you hate doing the dishes? How about a bright reminder above the sink to remind you why you're doing this financial thing? Do you love watching T.V.? Perhaps a sticky note next to it will excite you about the task you've set yourself. Pick spots and put these little pieces of you all over your house. Claim the space. Take up space. Fill your home with hopes for the future to drive out ghosts from your past.

The Chinese say, "A picture is worth a thousand words."

William James, the father of American psychology, stressed that the subconscious mind will bring to pass any picture held in mind and backed by faith. Act as though I am, and I will be. (Murphy, 2011, p. 80)

I know this period in your financial life is extremely rough; I've been there. Trying to find your feet is terrible when the person who's always stood by your side has left and you're dealing with your emotions *and* finances.

However, you need to get up and fight your way out of both emotional trauma and financial trauma. That's why, once you figure out where you stand financially, you must set goals to start working toward fixing those finances. At times, you will feel low and lost. Be prepared for these feelings. Fix your eyes on your dream, and let your goals be those constant pushes, those little things you know you can do even when you lose the strength to continue. Set SMART goals, plan your success roadmap, and feel excited about the process.

Remember that the attempt matters more than the success. You're new to the field, and so are 50% of the women in America. Things can and will happen; you must take them in stride with determination and resilience.

You've got this! It's not a race, and it's never the end of the line as long as you have a goal to work toward, no matter how small. Remember to pick yourself up, dust yourself off, and keep going when the road detours or becomes a little bumpy.

Chapter Exercises and Reflections

In this chapter, we've talked a lot about setting goals and how you'll use that to keep you motivated, so let's go over the steps.

First, define your **dream.** Picture it clearly, and draw it. This will make it seem more real and achievable.

If it's a house, where is it? What sort of roof will it have? What color are the walls? Will you keep a pet in it? Draw it out.

If it's your dream job, what position will you have? How many people will work under you? Where will your office be? Which company will it be with? What will your work table look like?

If it's a business, what will you name it? Where will your shop be? Will your friends come to visit you in your building? How many employees will you have?

Ask yourself all of these questions and draw the answers. It doesn't have to be perfectly artistic; it just has to be what you see on paper, however you want it to be. Keep this at your bedside or on the wall—this is your treasured goal.

Next up, set your **long-term goals.** Figure out what you'll do to reach those goals. We've already looked at a template that follows the SMART goal-setting method. Fill in the blanks, and your goal will be set:

"I will ___________ *(the target)* by doing ____________ *(steps to reach the target)* by ___________ *(deadline)."*

Now, for **short-term goals**. You set your long-term goal; now, set out your short-term goals and the roadmap to get you to the long-term goal. Please ensure they are SMART (Specific. Measurable. Attainable. Realistic. Timely).

Last but not least, feel excited about your work! You've planned for the numbers at this point, but now go crazy with what you're good at—drawing, writing, collages, anything that will help make your goals visual. Put these up on the walls and anywhere prominent. Plan it as if you believe it! Below each reminder note you make for yourself, add a doodle or picture of the treat you'll give yourself after you've achieved it. Do whatever it takes!

"I cradled my head in my hands as I contemplated my Big Financial Dream not to live with my parents after my divorce. It felt huge and unattainable at that moment. To ensure moving in with my parents didn't happen, I needed to devise a plan and not just leave it all to fate. Because of my shortened timeline, my goal of a new home was actually a short-term goal. 'I will be completely moved out of our house and into a new home (not with my parents) for my two dogs

and me by the end of November.' Now, to make that a reality with some shorter-term goals."

Chapter 4:

Rebuilding Your Financial Foundation: Create Your Post-Divorce Budget

"When I was confronted with all my expenses, I wanted to throw a tantrum, yell, and rant at the world for making things so difficult. But realistically, this was my new life without my husband, and I needed to pull myself together. I knew the world would only help me live better if I tried to help myself."

In Chapters 2 and 3, we studied the importance of knowing your financial status and setting goals accordingly. Change and progress take time. You won't reach your goals instantly, but you can begin to progress steadily toward them by prioritizing specific goals. To know which goals to prioritize, you must adopt an essential tool: budgeting.

Often, we lose track of our earnings and money outflow. Think about the rising price of groceries, kids' extracurriculars, and a little misplaced leisure and luxury spending. Please don't be shy or embarrassed; it happens to everyone. We are human, and wanting to make yourself and your kids happy is natural.

This chapter examines the habit of budgeting in great detail and provides insight into its importance and impact on living a better lifestyle and reaching your goals and dreams. Wouldn't it be better to feel more confident in your life, knowing you can support yourself rather than experience anxiety every time you receive another bill? Of course it would!

Why Budget?

Budgeting, in its most basic definition, provides the tools for planning how to use your money to make beneficial financial decisions and reduce unnecessary stress. It will help you choose based on your financial interests while remaining financially stable ("What is," 2022). Budgeting has multiple benefits for aiding your transition to an independent life.

When you have a clear view of your income, assets, and liabilities, you can adjust your lifestyle and financial decisions according to your budgeting plans. It's empowering to make financial decisions according to your interests; however, knowing you've made a well-thought-out and well-informed choice to spend or save money is even more empowering. Of course, for some, changing your lifestyle may seem like a letdown, but remember that things won't be this way forever. You'll work toward a better future when you set up, manage, and maintain a reasonable budget.

After a divorce, you may fall into a habit of irresponsible spending, either as a means of coping or trying to rebuild your old lifestyle. Panic can engulf you if you don't have a checklist and plan to move forward.

Imagine yourself in a forest without a map. The sun is setting, and you must escape before dark. As the forest grows darker, you find yourself lost, hungry, and trapped in fear. Stumbling about with no clear path or direction only drives you deeper into the forest and deeper into your fear. A light and a map to mark the shortcuts would go a long way toward helping you out of that dark and scary forest.

Following your divorce, your financial life might resemble the forest I described. You feel lost and trapped in fear as you sort through your bills and expenses, trying to decide when and how you're going to pay them while at the same time saving for emergencies, vacation, college, and retirement. You feel there is no clear path or light to find your way out.

A budget is the light and the map out of your financial forest. With a budget, you will no longer be stumbling in the dark but will be able to make sound financial decisions that will aid you in obtaining the goals you set earlier.

When faced with financial stress, you feel overwhelmed and tired. It's mentally exhausting to take care of so many things at once. Still, with the mighty power of budgeting, you can make proactive decisions and feel empowered as your checklist begins to shrink and your goals become clear and focused. ("Importance of a Post-Divorce," 2023).

Creating a Basic Budget

There are six easy steps you can follow to create a basic budget aimed at helping you manage your finances:

Step 1: Calculate Your Net Income

Most people want to focus on total salary rather than the actual income coming home after taxes, retirement deductions, and insurance withholdings. Net income is the money that goes into your bank account and is available to spend every month. If you own your own business, it depends on whether you pay yourself a wage or take money out as an owner draw. If you receive wages from your company, your net income is once again the money deposited into your bank account from your paycheck. If you take an owner draw, it is the monthly amount you take out of your business to pay yourself.

If your net income changes every month, look back at the past 12 months and use a monthly average. This net income will be the amount you use when drawing up your budget.

Step 2: Track Your Expenditures

Now that you have a good grasp on the amount of money coming in, where is it going?

Tracking your money outlay is the primary task for Step 2. Create a list of the categories you spend money on for the month, such as rent, utilities, groceries, insurance, vehicle expenses, entertainment, etc. For three months, track your expenses and purchases in each category to see how you spend your money. Write down EVERYTHING you spend money on: your rent, utilities, groceries, even that cup of coffee at the coffee shop, or the pack of gum you picked up when you got gas. Write it down if you bought it with your credit or debit card (or check if that's how you roll). Write it down if you bought it with cash from the ATM. Write it down even if you bought it with the change you found in your sofa.

If you need to develop a solid budget sooner, go back to your bank and credit card statements for the last three months and write down everything you spent during that time. Obviously, anything you paid cash for won't be caught up in this net, so this "looking back" method may not work if you use cash often. If that's the case, start writing everything down starting TODAY. It will still make you aware of how you spend your money.

Step 3: Set Your Goals

The third step to setting a budget is organizing the short and long-term goals we discussed earlier. These goals may include saving for a house downpayment or your child's education, starting a retirement fund, settling debts, or paying off credit card debt. With your goals in front of you to keep you motivated, it'll be easier to cut down on your spending if necessary.

Step 4: Make a Plan

This step requires you to look at everything with a critical eye. What's the game plan here? Are you looking for a place where you can cut back to live within your income? Are you creating a savings plan for a future, well-deserved vacation? Or are you mapping out how you will pay down your credit card debt?

Several methods of budgeting can help you manage your finances. When choosing a budgeting method, the most important thing to consider is to select the one you will stick with and do every day. Here are a few ideas:

Zero-based Budget

This budget plan caters to those with a set monthly income who know all their monthly expenses.

The process is simple. Take your calculated net income and subtract the monthly expenditures you tracked earlier, allocating a certain amount for each category. Make sure you have included a category for your budget goals, such as allocating an additional amount to your credit card debt repayment every month or saving a specific amount to your savings account for the downpayment on your dream home. Your end total should always equal zero. If you find yourself short, you must find where to cut back and make adjustments. If you have leftover money, it goes into your savings account for a rainy day.

This method allows you to adjust your budget for a particular category by reducing the money from one budget category and adding it to another category. The main requirement is to make sure the equation results in zero.

Net Income - Monthly Expenditures = Zero.

The Pay Yourself First Budget

This strategy is for people who struggle to set money aside in savings—in essence, those who spend every penny they earn each month and often wonder why they can't save.

The "Pay Yourself First" plan requires you to set aside a portion of your income to save or invest first while using the rest for monthly living expenses. Setting aside a separate portion first thing means you're less likely to run short of money for saving and investing when paying monthly debts and expenses.

It would be best if you still had a good grasp of your monthly outflow to set a reasonable amount to pay yourself for your savings and investing. You don't want to run out of money for the month before you've paid the phone bill or made that additional credit card payment.

The Envelope "Cash-Based" Budget

This budget works best for those struggling to stay within each category's allocation. It is a cash-based plan that mimics the zero-based plan but with actual physical cash separated into different envelopes according to your monthly expenditure categories. You will have separate envelopes for gas, groceries, entertainment, etc., containing the amount of money you have budgeted for that particular category. That is the ONLY envelope you will use when purchasing within that category. Take money out of the gas envelope only to pay for gas for the month. You never take cash from the other envelopes due to falling short in any category. Your top priorities should be groceries, utilities, insurance, and rent/mortgage.

Note: In today's cashless payment environment, you can set up your "envelopes" in a digital spreadsheet. However, this requires considerably more awareness and effort to avoid overspending your envelope. I recommend this only if you are highly motivated and dedicated to staying within your plan. You can also implement a hybrid system by setting up your spreadsheet for those categories that aren't cash-friendly, such as mortgage, insurance, utilities, etc., while still using physical envelopes for those more cash-friendly categories, like gas, groceries, and entertainment.

The 50/30/20 Budget

This plan requires you to break your income down into three categories:

- o Needs and Obligations such as mortgage/rent, utilities, and car payments: 50%
- o Wants like travel, concerts, and eating out: 30%
- o Savings and Debt Payments: 20%

Although this method is easy, I do not recommend it for new budgeters, as it is easy to miscategorize spending. For example, I see debt repayment, such as payments on credit cards, student loans, and vehicles, as an obligation (Category 1), but additional payments to credit cards or personal loans to meet your debt reduction goals are considered Category 3. Another example might be new shoes. It could be a want if you have other shoes to wear, but it could be a need if your kiddos have outgrown theirs and you have no choice but to buy new ones.

You will still need to do some math (and not "girl-math," actual math-math) to figure out exactly how much of your income to allocate to each category, and I highly recommend tracking it through a spreadsheet to ensure you're staying within your budget.

This plan may not be ideal for people with higher debt or savings goals, although you can tweak the percentages to fit your net income.

The No Budget Budget

Simply put, save up and spend according to your current means. Track your income and account balances through budgeting apps, note recurring bills, set aside a portion for savings and debts, and spend the rest whenever and however you see fit without becoming overdrawn.

Although it's essential to track in all of the budgets, the "No Budget Budget" is the one that can get you in all sorts of trouble. It's the one where it's the easiest to overspend because each time you go to spend money, you have convinced yourself it is okay. But it is NOT okay if you buy that new purse when you haven't paid for groceries for the entire month or the phone bill has slipped your mind. It's super easy to run out of money on this budget before you've run out of month.

A key thing to remember with this budget plan is when to hold back and tell yourself no. It isn't easy, but you must try (Chafin et al., 2023).

Step 5: Stay On Your Budget

In this step, write down your wants and find where you can cut back. What things can you set aside for later? Do you really need to buy that new dress right now? Perhaps you can set it aside for a bit and use the money you would spend to pay down your credit card a little bit faster.

Once you've checked your wants, check your needs to see if they are actual needs or things you've convinced yourself you need. Maybe you could part with some of them or cut back on others. An example might be to ask yourself if you really need to buy that particular brand of coffee every month or if you can find some good, budget-friendly alternatives.

Step 6: Regularly Review Your Budget

Check in on your budget frequently to ensure you're sticking to your plan. Most things remain the same, but sometimes you get a raise at work or you receive a notice your insurance payments are increasing. Reviewing your budgeting plan will help you adjust accordingly (Habits, 2024).

Time is a-wastin'; better get started on this budget thing as soon as possible so you can achieve your dreams even faster.

Here's a really great place to go to look for some budgeting templates that might strike your fancy: https://www.notion.so/templates/category/budgets

Identify Variable Expenses

Don't you hate it when you meticulously track your grocery bills and set money aside in an envelope for them, only to go to the grocery store and feel you did not leave with enough groceries to last an entire month?

"When did the prices get so high? This wasn't so expensive before!"

This is an example of a variable expense or something with fluctuating prices. Yeah, yeah, I know. It's another headache to deal with, but we can't ignore it now, can we?

Variable expenses may include:

- groceries,
- gas,
- clothing,
- travel expenses,
- entertainment, and so on.

You have no control over these variations, which often disturb or throw your budget off balance. However, with certain actions, you can adjust your budget accordingly.

First, separate your fixed expenses from your variable expenses. Then you will know exactly how much of your income to direct toward fulfilling the fixed costs and how much to set up for the variable expenses (keeping their fluctuating nature in mind).

You can follow the budgeting methods mentioned earlier to categorize your budget items and accommodate these changes. You can also use tracking apps or spreadsheets to review your budget and monthly spending (Schwahn, 2023).

Set Your Budget Categories

I mentioned earlier that we must separate our needs from our wants. In more formal terms, this means creating two categories: essential and non-essential expenses.

Essential expenses are vital in ensuring a standard and basic lifestyle at the very least. This means things such as groceries, utilities, rent, debt payment, electricity, heating, commuting, and similar things.

Non-essential expenses include things that contribute to your leisure, such as entertainment and impulse purchases. These expenses might consist of concerts, dining out, pets, and, to a certain extent, personal care. (Hey, I'm all for self-care, but maybe picking out products from the pricier end of the shelf is not the best way to go about things, especially if it will leave you financially constrained).

The easiest way to do this is to record your expenses and label them into one of the two categories. Then, you can see where you can reduce non-essential expenditures to contribute more to your savings, investing, or paying down debt.

To reduce non-essential costs, use tricks like negotiating for discounts, using coupons, and possibly branching out to more affordable and local products to lower your rate of cash outflow. You can also eliminate unnecessary subscriptions you discover during your expense reconnaissance. Soon, with monthly budget reviews, you'll be on a proactive track to a brighter future (Ashwinsk, n.d.).

Plan For The Future

It is just as important to think about the future as the present, and you will only have complete financial security if you begin to think this way. With long-term goals, such as purchasing a better home, saving for retirement, and setting aside funds for emergencies, you will surely build a secure future for yourself. With a budget, you set your priorities and put aside funds for each goal, ensuring you deal with the essential things first and then move on to others, such as repaying your debts.

Allocate Funds For Savings And Emergencies

Setting aside funds for emergencies and savings provides a safety net in case you face emergencies or events such as medical bills or car breakdowns.

Let me tell you that facing medical emergencies without having enough to pay for them is the most horrific and vulnerable feeling in the world, but budgeting will help you t prepare yourself beforehand. God forbid you should ever face such a situation, but you can never be too prepared for such a possibility. Imagine the relief and confidence you'll have knowing an emergency won't put you or your family in a difficult financial situation.

There is no set amount of savings to meet every situation, but as a rough estimate, you are advised to save around three to six times your monthly expenses. The calculations are easy. You have already listed your monthly expenses and debt payments. Sum it up and multiply it by how many months you wish to target. The result will give you the rough amount of funds you should have in your savings for emergencies. Be prepared to adjust this amount according to any changes in your life, such as a fluctuating income (you might need more emergency funds in this case), a sudden medical emergency, or an accident.

Here are some strategies to help you save up some money for emergencies:

Practical First Steps

Calculate your monthly expenses to see where you can cut down. You can also increase your income by working extra paid hours or picking up a freelancing gig, whatever makes the most sense to you and your situation. Remember not to bite off more than you can chew. After all, you still have kids to raise and dogs to walk!

Make It A Priority

Treat your emergency funds as a high-priority category in your budget. Set aside a monthly amount and track your budget using spreadsheets and tracking apps to ensure smooth progress.

Consistency

Scheduling an automatic transfer from your checking account to your savings account will make your life easier and save you time vs. setting aside funds manually. This way, you won't even have to think about it, and the next thing you know, your emergency funds will have grown, seemingly on their own.

The Highs And The Lows

Often, we get into the habit of splurging the moment extra money comes our way, such as bonuses or tax refunds, but the key is to make sure you don't go crazy and blow it all. It's time to be responsible and save some extra cash. You never know when life will hit you with one of its 'downs' or 'lows,' so it's best to be prepared beforehand.

Saving Accounts

Here is a list of savings accounts you can use to build up your emergency funds:

- **High-Yields Savings Account:** A high-interest account that will help your funds grow. With this, your funds will be available whenever you need it.
- **Money Market Account:** This is a combination savings and checking account, allowing you to experience high interest rates with the ability to take out emergency funds by writing checks.
- **Certificate of Deposit:** Your emergency savings will be locked until the certificates mature, but this method guarantees a higher interest rate. (I only recommend this

option if you have additional savings in a readily available account).

Things to Consider

Try not to go crazy by focusing on the interest rates and focus more on the availability of your funds. When facing an emergency, you'll be more grateful to have the funds in your hands and ready for use rather than having them locked in for a fixed amount of time. Weigh each option's pros and cons and availability to make the best choice according to your needs and requirements.

You can choose between traditional and online banking based on convenience and preference. If these decisions are difficult, try contacting a financial advisor with professional experience to guide you through the process.

Positive Effects

Not only will having available emergency funds ease your mind against the fear of not having enough to face emergencies, but it will also boost your confidence when making proactive decisions and believing that you can be financially independent and make good decisions. With your growing emergency funds and savings, you'll feel prepared for unforeseen circumstances without compromising the funds you set up for your future goals. As long as you remain consistent and build up these funds again if you ever have to use them, there is no doubt you'll be able to fulfill your financial goals ("Emergency Savings," 2024).

Tracking Your Spending

I've mentioned budgeting tools and apps plenty of times, but now, I'll provide you with a list of apps you can use and their benefits.

YNAB For Hands-On Zero Budgeting

YNAB works best for those who enjoy hands-on experiences. It supplies resources for learning about budgeting while teaching you how to use the app. You are required to input your income and separate the net value into the categories you set up as your expenses. It also lets you connect your savings and checking accounts, making you proactive with your financial decisions. However, you'll have to commit to reviewing your budget when using this app.

GoodBudget For Hands-On Envelope Budgeting

This app follows the envelope budgeting system, where you portion your income according to your categories, called envelopes. A downside is that you can't connect your bank account to the app, so you must enter your account balance and every expense or purchase. If this seems tedious, the GoodBudget app is probably not your best solution.

EveryDollar For Simple Zero-Based Budgeting

The free version of EveryDollar does not sync accounts, so you'll need to enter the inflow and outflow of money, set reminders, and adjust categories in your budget on your own. However, the pricey premium version does connect to your bank account. It automatically records your income and expenditures and offers advice to move forward according to your preferences. It also connects to your savings and investing accounts.

Empower Personal Dashboard For Tracking Wealth and Spending

As an investing app, the free version provides tools to customize lists and mark expenditures and transactions. It also allows you to monitor your savings and checking accounts, credit cards, and other accounts by connecting them to the app. However, its tools for budgeting are limited, as it is predominantly an investing app.

PocketGuard For A Simplified Budgeting Snapshot

This app connects your accounts, credit cards, loans, investments, and bills to offer a hands-off experience. It monitors them and shows you your net worth and remaining capital after saving money for necessities. The paid version provides a debt payment plan. As it does so much for you, those wishing to make proactive budgeting decisions might prefer to use something other than this app.

NerdWallet For 50/30/20 budgeting

This app, which includes budget planners, spreadsheets, and calculators, allows you to monitor money flow, net worth, and debt while helping you maintain a budget using the 50/30/20 method (Ayoola, 2024).

Take a moment to map out which features you will need and the budgeting plan you wish to follow. Then, do your homework and pick out the app that will suit you best.

Adjusting Your Budget As Needed

We've talked about adjusting our budget before. We all know that age-old saying that "life has its ups and downs," but I know damn well that we'd all rather be living in a constant state of highs than ever feel the lows. Then again, for some of us, divorce is one of the biggest lows life could give us. But do you know what's worse? Drowning in debt, and that is something we simply aren't going to do.

Here are some tips:

- A bonus or raise at work does not mean it's splurge time or a trip to that fancy boutique down the block. It means setting 50% aside for savings, emergency funds, or debt payment and 50% to spend or save as you see fit.
- Separate the wants from the needs. What you want is not what you need, and until it becomes imperative for survival, it should be placed on your low-priority list.
- Reduce credit card debt by opting out of using your cards. Otherwise, you may not notice how much you're spending until the bill shows up.

- For a change as significant as divorce and whatever follows, you'll need to revisit your budget plan and edit it so you'll be able to accommodate the new changes in your life. If you can't support the lifestyle you wish to have, then make that a long-term goal and save up for it while trying to stay happy with your current lifestyle.

Remember that you are courageous enough to stay strong, doing things against your comfort level to live and value life, even in the simplest ways ("Adjusting Your Budget," 2019).

Long-Term Financial Planning

Setting long-term goals will point you in the right direction when setting up a budget to maintain financial independence. Long-term goals also serve as a benchmark for seeing how far you've come on your journey. They can also help free you from debt and retire peacefully. There are many types of long-term goals. Some include:

- **Sign Up For A Retirement Plan**

This strategy will help you save during your career, and once you retire, you'll have a reasonable sum of money to support your lifestyle in retirement. I recommend finding a financial planner to work with when deciding on the best retirement plans.

- **Finance A Vacation**

Saving up for a vacation will allow you to relax and take a break from working without worrying about your finances taking a dip. Take some time to save because what is a vacation if you can't enjoy it by spending time enjoying the sights, eating food, and buying souvenirs?

- **Resolve Student Loan Debt**

Whether you have student loan debt looming or you've been paying it for some time, it's best to remove this shadow as soon as possible.

When your student loan has gone away, you will experience a whole other feeling of freedom.

- **Settle Credit Card Debt**

Make a goal of not adding to your credit card debt. Instead, focus on saving or separating portions of your income to pay off this debt. Avoid paying for expensive purchases with your credit card, and instead, focus on spending according to your monthly income.

- **Become a Homeowner**

Another source of motivation can be improving your living conditions. Set aside funds for moving to a new place, whether it be another city, the suburbs, or even a new country! You'll feel accomplished once you find your dream home and can afford it independently.

- **College Tuition**

With growing kids, you must always remember that they may soon pursue higher education at a college or university. To prepare beforehand, start building a fund for their college fees now. With this safety net, you'll never panic about needing more to help with your kids' education. Check in with your financial planner to find the best way to start this savings plan.

- **Reserve for Emergencies**

Keeping an emergency fund is a great way to prevent tumbling into more debt. Trust me, we don't want any more of that. Save up and contribute a portion of your income to your emergency fund so that, no matter what happens, if you need money, you can rely on your savings rather than taking out another loan.

- **Find a Higher Paying Job**

As time passes, you may be expanding your scope in your chosen field and looking for opportunities with a higher salary. Consider improving your resume with extra courses or requesting a salary raise from your employer. If you are self-employed, consider expanding your business by investing or hiring employees.

- **Financial Freedom**

This is your endgame: spend without fearing you'll run out of money, make sound financial decisions as if they're second nature, and no longer worry about how to divide or save the next month's income so you don't have to compromise your wants. It means finally living the lifestyle you've dreamed of and fulfilling your children's dreams without letting them forget the obstacles you've overcome to get there.

I could write an entire book on examples of long-term goals, but I'll leave the rest up to you to decide. Use your budgeting skills to plan for a peaceful and satisfying future in which the worries of finance no longer remain ("Finance Goals," 2023).

This chapter was heavy, with a lot of information, but I'd be lying if I said it was unimportant. My goal is to ensure that none of you suffer the way I did and are prepared to take on the world as independent women.

I'm not saying you can't ask for help, but you must also try to help yourself first. STAY STRONG, and keep these tips and tricks in mind. Take control and be powerful with the hold you'll have over your future. Use this same confidence to move forward and learn more about becoming truly financially independent.

"Facing up to the reality of my financial life immediately following my divorce was disheartening, to say the least. I'd spent so much time in my marriage taking care of my kids and family that I hadn't moved forward in my business and career. I was in no way prepared to suddenly be covering all life's expenses, and in my 50's to boot. Although I didn't have much debt, I still needed to take stock of what I owed and to whom. More importantly, I needed to be aware of my

monthly expenses and, most importantly, be prepared to up my income game."

Chapter 5:

Navigating the Debt Maze—A Strategic Guide to Managing Debt

"Coming out of my second divorce, I was fortunate enough not to have a tremendous amount of debt. However, my first divorce (yup, remember I told you I've been through the divorce dance TWICE) saddled me with more debt than I could even comprehend. I had credit card debt, small business loan debt, and a car payment ... and I still had to meet all the day-to-day and month-to-month expenses and provide for my two small children. So, I sat down with my budget, did all the maneuvering of money, and put different amounts in different categories. I listed out my needs and my wants. I agonized over paying my debts and came up with plan after plan. But no matter how I brainstormed my finances, there was just no way all that debt would get paid with the amount of money my business was making. The monthly interest was adding up too fast, and I knew I had to do something drastic. With my heart in my mouth and my hat in my hand, I contacted a bankruptcy attorney. It was my best decision, but I swore to myself I would never go through that humiliating experience again."

Managing finances becomes all the more difficult when hidden costs and debt repayment creep up on you like the poisonous Devil's Snare, eating away at your earnings before you even get a chance to budget for the groceries, leaving you utterly bewildered wondering where all your income went.

- *"But I earned so much! Why can't I afford to take the kids to the zoo this month?"*
- *"Wait... more debt?"*
- *"I've spent twice as much as this project was estimated, and they're asking for MORE?"*
- *"How on earth do I buy more things when the* ***interest*** *from the old purchases is eating away at me?"*
- *"I'm practically broke before I begin spending!"*

According to ancient writer Publilius Syrus, "Debt is the slavery of the free" (Updike, 2023). You may feel overwhelmed by your debt—almost enslaved—because you've lost control over where your money is going. It's as if you're dependent on someone else's money (because you are), and you worry that they will come knocking on your door any day now, wanting it all back. But you have nothing left to give.

As many of us know, the feeling is acutely painful. However, it isn't just you. The average 18- to 29-year-old in America owes $12,871, and the average 30- to 39-year-old owes a whopping $26,532 (Fay, 2023).

Everywhere you look, people are feeling the burden that comes with being in debt.

Although fighting debt is an uphill battle, you can weather it with persistence. You've been through a rough divorce, and you might be deep in debt for the first time in your life, experiencing this helplessness for the first time and feeling utterly lost. However, as I've said before, you must focus on being patient with yourself.

Here's what may have happened: you desperately needed money to pay basic expenses. Perhaps you've overspent because you didn't know how to manage your finances. You promised yourself you'd pay it back soon, but when you tried, the amount had gone through the roof with the added interest.

Perhaps you've added to it with shared debt from before your divorce. As you paid off the immediate interest, you had to buy more essentials, incurring more debt, and so it continued until now … when you find yourself deeply entrenched and overwhelmed.

Does that sound familiar? If so, it's time to liberate yourself from those shackles. In this chapter, we will look at how you can work on debt management efficiently so you can breathe freely and live fearlessly.

Assessing Your Debt Situation

In the same way you assessed your financial situation earlier (how much you own), now's the time to determine how much you owe. Keep these figures separate. With all the different interest rates, credit cards, and creditors, you may have many accounts to settle, and at this stage, you are simply taking inventory of your debt.

Credit Card Balances

The first thing to do is look at your credit cards. There are three numbers to look for. The first is your credit card **balance**, the total outstanding balance telling you how much you owe the creditor. Second, you'll need the **interest rate**, a percentage that tells you how much they add to your balance with each billing cycle. The higher the interest rate, the more your balance will increase. This number is sometimes labeled as the **APR,** the **Annual Percentage rate.** You pay interest monthly in this case, too, but the APR tells you how much you'll pay if you keep the debt over the entire year. Thirdly, you need to know the **minimum payment**, the minimum amount you *must* pay before the due date. If you miss this, they add late payment fees, reduce promotional offers, and lower your credit score. This number changes monthly, so watch out for it!

There are several ways to check your credit card balance. Use the number on the back of your credit card to call the company. They'll need to know your account number, phone number, or Social Security number, but that's normal. Ask for your balance, your credit card limit, the minimum payment, and their interest rates, and note them down. Your second option is to create an online account on your card issuer's website or app and log in to check these values. If you use this method, secure your account by adding a double-check system so the app will ask for your face ID or fingerprint and password, for example. Third, check the paperwork to get your numbers if you've signed up for paper notifications. These notifications are sent out before every new payment is due.

Add your balance, credit limit, and interest rates to your accounting info using whatever method is convenient. Each card's numbers may differ, so watch out for that, too (Perkins-Southam, 2021).

Loans and Other Obligations

After figuring out your credit card debt, look deeper into the loans you have taken out. These can include

- student loans
- mortgage loans
- home equity loans
- credit builder loans
- debt consolidation loans
- payday loans
- small business loans
- family loans (VanSomeren, 2021).

These are loans you might have taken out in the past that are collecting interest or short-term loans you've amassed because you desperately needed money but didn't have good credit after your divorce. In any case, you've borrowed the money, and it must be returned. Put the amounts into your accounting info, and right next to them, add the interest rate.

We'll work through what everything means in more detail in a while;

but at this point, you need to sit down and confront these numbers *bravely*. I know you may not be used to finances and debts. I know these numbers are demons you want to ignore because you know they'll overwhelm you, but you need to face them properly. Just do this once so you can get to their roots and devise a plan to finish them off.

Everyone who's been through it knows and understands. If you have a trusted friend or relative who has been in your shoes, ask them for advice and, if needed, look to them for motivation.

"Remember, the hardest part is showing up, but you can do it" (Mishler, 2021).

In showing up for yourself with your accounting info, you're proving you're ready to fight, that you're much stronger than all those who live with the loans until the creditors take everything from them.

Categorizing debt

The first category of debt is **unsecured** loans. These are personal or other loans based on your signature alone. They include credit cards because they have been issued based on your reliability. These creditors trust you but often ask for substantial interest rates in return. Because of their high interest rates, these loans eat away at your income like nothing else, so make getting rid of them your priority.

The second category is **secured** loans. This type of loan is given to you by the lender based on some type of **collateral**. For example, you might have given the lender ownership title to your car or the deed to your house in return for the loan. However, if you fail to pay the lender, the vehicle or house legally becomes theirs, and there's not much you can do about it. These loans usually sport a lower interest rate than unsecured loans, but you'll lose something far more valuable if you ignore them.

If you're in a situation where you have both kinds of loans, you need to prioritize paying off the high-interest loans to have more control over your earnings. However, you must still watch out for secured loans because their deadlines are more critical.

In short, whatever extra money you have after paying for the necessities in your budget (including payments on secured loans like mortgages and car loans and minimum payments on unsecured loans like credit cards), apply it to the top loan on your list according to one of the strategies below.

Creating a Debt Repayment Plan

Earlier, we discussed creating a financial plan and setting money aside for debt repayment as a financial goal. Now, you make it a properly defined goal with sub-steps. To help you, I will introduce two strategies you can implement during your planning process. Each strategy can be broken down into smaller goals using the SMART method. The strategies I share here will help you prioritize your debt repayments.

The Debt Snowball Strategy

This strategy encourages you to pay off your smaller debts before moving on to bigger ones. It will reduce the number of debts you must keep track of, and you can celebrate when you complete each one. However, you must pay off the minimum amount on all your other debts to avoid fines.

If you decide on this method, rearrange your outstanding loans according to size, targeting the smaller ones first while making the minimum payments on everything else. Trust me, crossing off smaller debts will be a gratifying experience.

The snowball method may help keep you motivated as it gives you reasons to celebrate in the initial phases of your divorce, when you may feel there's little to be happy about. You also don't need to worry about APRs, monthly interest amounts, or do much accounting, which can be a relief if you need to learn more about finances. However, it could also mean you end up paying extra on interest, and your overall debt may last longer, as the smaller debts are not necessarily the ones with the highest interest rates.

The Debt Avalanche Strategy

This strategy first targets the debt with the highest interest rate. Using the Debt Avalance Strategy, you'll save more money as you will pay less overall interest. However, remember that you still need to make minimum payments on all other debts to avoid late payment charges, or you risk the entire note being called due (and possibly losing your collateral). In any case, rearrange the outstanding amounts in your accounting list based on the descending order of interest rates so you'll know which ones to tackle first.

This method helps you pay off debt faster and pay less, but you won't have the satisfaction of quickly reducing the number of creditors on your list. Moreover, if you have high balances on higher-interest loans, you might be stuck paying off the same loan for quite some time. You will, however, have the satisfaction of knowing that you're doing the most efficient thing.

Here's an example to help you understand the two options I've shared:

Let's say you have these figures

- $3,000 surplus money every month after paying the minimum amounts
- $10,000 debt on your credit card at an APR of 18.99%
- $9,000 for a car loan at a 3.00% interest rate
- $15,000 in student loans at a 4.50% interest rate

Using the **snowball method**, you'd pay off the car loan first because it's the smallest amount. This would take you around three months. Then, you would go for the others. The overall interest you'd pay would be $1,514.97 over 11 months.

Conversely, credit card debt would be targeted first using the **avalanche method** as it has the highest interest rate. This way, you'll be debt-free in 11 months, paying $1,011.60 in interest.

The payment period is approximately the same when comparing the two, but you'll pay $500 extra with the snowball method (Eneriz, 2023). Remember that, in both cases, paying the minimum amount is a priority.

The bottom line is that both methods work for different kinds of people.

I've introduced you to both so you can choose what will work best for you. If you're good at being consistent without needing immediate rewards and you're good at budgeting, go for the avalanche method. You'll save money and be debt-free sooner.

However, if you need to see that things are progressing because you're on the brink of giving up, use the snowball method; it'll help motivate you to keep going. I have had clients (and done it myself) that fluctuate back and forth depending on what works best for their emotional state at the time. This is not a race, and there's no pressure. Be honest with your decision; you must be more consistent than efficient here.

Negotiating With Creditors

One of the most terrifying aspects of a divorce is the people who come to your door or call you to deliver threats to make you cough up money you don't have—money you've promised to pay them. It's understandable if you feel like burying your head in the sand and ignoring the overwhelming fear and failure gripping you.

Even after you make your debt repayment plan, you might still feel overwhelmed and unable to repay that money. The good news is that you can call your creditors to renegotiate your debt if you're ready to be proactive and change your situation.

Now, you're probably asking, *"Why on Earth would the company be okay with giving me concessions?"*

The answer's pretty simple: if you're months behind in your payments and on the brink of bankruptcy, it's likely you won't be paying them back at all. Moreover, they also want you to get current on your debt because pestering you constantly costs them money. The bottom line is that you should know they *are* likely to help out and that there is a chance for you.

With this understanding, let's talk about the *how*.

One option is to negotiate a **lower monthly payment** on the balance. First, calculate how much you can reasonably afford to pay monthly on the loan. Try to keep this figure at least 50% of the original payment with a fixed amount of time to repay the loan. The amount and payment time allotted must be realistic because your credit score will suffer if you miss a single payment after negotiations.

Another option is to **renegotiate the actual amount of the loan**. Come up with a lump sum you know you can reasonably afford to pay the lender to forgive the rest of the loan. As I said, the creditor wants to negotiate and reduce their potential losses, so you could begin by offering 30% of the total debt as a lump sum. If they refuse, increase the lump sum amount you're offering to pay up to 50% of the outstanding debt (making sure you can pay that amount). If they ask you to pay a more considerable lump sum, try negotiating a lower monthly payment or start negotiations with a different creditor to see if you can reduce that loan amount. Remember, you have some leverage in the situation, so use it.

During the negotiations, it is essential to state *why* you could not pay off the debt in the first place. Your creditors will likely understand since thousands of people are in your situation. Tell them about your divorce, and be honest and open about it. It's a difficult situation, and the company representative is likely to understand that you have a valid reason, and they will be able to trust you in the future.

If the creditor doesn't understand, you must know your rights under the Fair Debt Collection Practices Act. Even if the negotiator is unfriendly, they cannot threaten you with arrest, say they're associated with the IRS, 'invent' debts you never took on, embarrass you in front of anyone, or harass you in any way. You're quite safe under the law, so be confident.

If creditors try to bully or belittle you, keep track of every phone call, email, or visit with negotiators, including their names, time and duration of call, tone of the conversation, and so on. These records will help if there's any trouble later. If you reach any agreements, have them in writing and sign them so they can't renege at the last minute. Be organized, and you're good to go.

If you need more motivation to pick up the phone and negotiate with your creditors, hear this: the credit company wants to get its money back before you file for bankruptcy and before it sells your debt to a collection company (often for much less than you owe them).

Your best bet is to go to the original creditor immediately. Prove that you're trying your best and have a plan to repay your debt, and you might be surprised at how willing they are to work with you. Prove you're irresponsible by burying your head in the sand and ignoring their phone calls, emails, and letters, and they'll start calling your note due and sending you to collections (which will leave a huge black eye on your credit report). On this dire note, I encourage you to take action post-haste.

It is understandable if you feel afraid to negotiate by yourself. As a last resort, you could approach a debt settlement company for help, but they will charge you heavily, so be careful and know how much you can afford to pay them (Shaw, 2022).

Negotiations are tricky, but they can help you look for the light at the end of this deep, terrifying tunnel. The only way forward is to fight your way ahead, so for this stage, you need to be brave *before* you begin to pay everything off consistently. If a few months of negotiations can spare you a lifetime of struggling under the heavy weight of debt, why not? The ball is in your court.

Limit Credit Card Use

I don't need to stress the need to limit the use of credit cards now that you know what a hassle it can be to dig your way out of debt. Using cards to pay off other debts can be tempting, especially when those "no interest for a year if you consolidate all your debt to our new card" offers roll in. But credit cards have unbelievably high interest rates. You might borrow a small amount, but due to the interest charged, it'll blow up into a massive sum quickly.

Consolidation and Refinancing Options

Up until now, we've looked at ways to deal with your creditors and how to manage all of them at the same time. However, there's yet another option: debt consolidation and refinancing. If you use these options, you will have to pay extra, but you might save yourself the time and effort needed to handle payments and negotiations with different creditors.

Consolidation

Debt consolidation involves combining all your debts into one account so you won't have to deal with different creditors. This method may help you manage your debt and even reduce the overall interest rate, but you must watch out for hidden charges.

If you're trying to consolidate debt for convenience's sake, know that nothing comes for free. Be sure to read the fine print carefully. If you decide to consolidate, make sure the interest you'll pay is lower than the total interest you would have been charged on all the individual loans. Remember to take into consideration the lender fees and any other charges for going to a new lender before you decide. Also, please double-check that you can manage the new monthly payment and that it fits your budget plan.

Another piece of advice: Ensure nothing valuable is used as collateral for your new consolidation loan. For example, consolidating all your debt into your house mortgage may be extremely risky because your entire house—a significant investment—is on the line.

When reconfiguring your budget for the new payment, leave some room to set aside money for emergencies. Regardless of the dire emergency, you can't afford to miss any payments on this type of loan. Once again, I remind you that nothing is free, so remember that while you look for the best consolidation plan.

Refinancing

Debt refinancing involves changing the current loan company to one with better repayment options, such as a lower interest rate or smaller monthly payment. It is not uncommon to consolidate and refinance your debt simultaneously, but as mentioned before, remember to watch out for new charges and make sure the overall interest rate and monthly payment work with your budget plan.

Since your emotions and reduced household earning capabilities may be draining your time and energy after your divorce, consider refinancing and consolidation options. When you need to make only one monthly payment, you won't forget to make minimum payments, you will be less likely to incur unnecessary fines, and you will save time tracing multiple debts. However, you may pay more interest for an extended period, so watch out for the duration, amount, and repayment terms. Also, ensure that if you've added collateral to the deal, you're not risking it by overestimating how much you can pay monthly. Please don't take risks; be realistic and do what it takes to keep things convenient and manageable while juggling so many things.

Prioritizing Financial Health

As Josh Billings—aka Henry Wheeler Shaw—once said, "Debt is like any other trap, easy enough to get into, but hard enough to get out of" ("Quote," 2022).

Debt is a curse and a burden that bends your back and ties your hands as it monopolizes your earnings. Taking up debt is an act of self-sabotage unless it's for a basic necessity you can't do without, like food or drinking water, and you should treat it as such.

Now, let's take another look at your budget. I want you to sit down and start crossing out stuff you don't immediately need. That sofa you've had your eyes on for the past year? It can wait. TV subscriptions can also wait, as can eating out, watching a movie, or shopping for fancy clothes. Cut down on anything unnecessary and replace it with cheaper options like watching a sunset or going for a walk. Trust me, they'll be as rewarding as the paid leisure activities once you get used to them, and the money you save can go toward debt repayment.

Seeking Professional Advice

Sometimes, getting out of debt can be too challenging to handle alone. You're not alone in being new to the financial field, and it's all right to be a beginner as long as you're willing to admit to it. If what I say here sounds too complicated, look for a professional to help you. Remember that this is about your unique journey and not about how your second-cousin's-best-friend's-aunt fished herself out of debt all by herself—it's okay to reach out.

Not only will seeking out a professional to help you understand what these financial terms mean be helpful, but it can also be highly motivational to talk to people who have seen so many others through this rough journey. Sometimes, a book cannot do as much as a face-to-face conversation, and it's okay to accept that.

Credit Counseling

A credit counselor is an agent who'll help you pay off your **unsecured** debts within a set time period. They can also help you with a debt management plan (DMP), contact creditors, design a financial plan, and negotiate to reduce interest rates and waive late fees.

They'll help you decide whether you want to go for the debt snowball or avalanche methods and how much you can pay monthly. They can also help you decide which option to use—whether debt consolidation or refinancing—and if it's feasible. In short, credit counseling will help you make all the decisions I've asked you to make and give you more personal tips on debt repayment. The objective is to save you from bankruptcy because that looks horrible on your credit score. Seems like an all-in-one solution, right?

On the flip side, I want you to remember—and this is perhaps Rule 1 of the financial world you've just been born into—that nothing comes for free. If something sounds too good, I want you to re-read the fine print, double-check the terms, and look for hidden fees and motives. Just because the company is nonprofit does *not* guarantee it will be free or affordable or that you will receive sincere service.

Beware of companies that ask for up-front fees. The Trade Commission forbids this, making it another red flag to watch out for. Knowing the terms of a financial deal is more important than blindly trusting an organization. If you have any doubts, call the state's attorney general's office or consumer protection agency to check if the company is legitimate.

Moreover, credit counseling will be a part of your credit report, so you won't be able to get more credit from the same creditors as before. This will prevent you from going deeper into debt, but it will further tie your hands if you need money in an emergency. Credit counseling is mostly only available to people who can meet at least their minimum payments, so make sure you can cover these.

If you need external help and can set aside the extra cash to pay their fees, here's how to find a company.

- Consult the National Foundation for Credit Counseling, a nonprofit organization that connects people with nonprofit credit counselors.
- Check with the U.S. Trustee Program's list of approved counselors. You'll have to consult with them by law before considering filing for bankruptcy.

Ask potential counselors about their services, how often you'll meet with them, their fees, free resources, financial help if you can't pay, the necessary documents and contracts, and their qualifications (Kagan, 2023).

Once you're satisfied with their credentials, you're good to go! Best of luck!

Bankruptcy

Bankruptcy is not for the faint of heart and should be looked into only as a last resort. A bankruptcy stays on your credit report for up to ten years and severely limits your ability to secure any financing if you need a new car or want to buy a house in the future. However, it will release you from your debts and stop any further interest, penalties, or late fees from accruing. You are no longer responsible for the monthly payment by releasing the debt. Be aware that a bankruptcy judge can liquidate your assets to pay off some of your creditors. In other words, you have much to lose if you choose this path. You may lose your car, and then how will you get to work? You may lose your home, and then you have to figure out a new place to live, which is much more difficult with a bankruptcy on your credit. It is best to attempt to renegotiate your debt or consolidate and refinance it first.

Emotional Aspects of Debt

In everything we've discussed, the one thing not to be underestimated when dealing with your post-divorce finances is your emotions. Divorce is not an easy event; it's an emotional ordeal. It's super easy to get overwhelmed with everything and slip into denial. I can't stress enough the importance of moving past your overwhelm and grief. Ignoring your creditors, racking up your credit card debt to pay daily expenses, and failing to make payments on loans is a recipe for disaster.

I get that indulging yourself right now is tempting. You've been through a HUGE emotional tsunami, and going out to eat because you're too tired to cook or surfing all the stuff on Amazon that would look cute in your new apartment is so much more fun than making budgets or talking to creditors. But being kind to yourself now by gorging on borrowed luxuries means being cruel to your future self, who will have to pay for them. That's not fair! Take a moment to understand the future emotional toll new debt will take on you and how you can deal with everything in a healthy, practical way.

As we've seen in the previous sections, debt can cripple your mental and emotional health because you deal with constant fear and uncertainty as you wonder:

- *"Will they take everything away from me?"*
- *"How many loans have I forgotten?"*
- *"How am I ever going to get out of this pathetic mess?"*
- *"Ugh... Wonder how long I have until the next person calls me and calls me a useless, poor, parasitic, no-good person?"*
- *"Why can't they just leave me alone?"*

Stress and anxiety will grip you. You'll sometimes wake up in the middle of the night, wondering how you will ever make it or if you'll ever be a good enough mother to support your children. This is inevitable, but you must face your fears and develop a debt reduction plan and a budget. Until you do that, you'll always be overwhelmed.

Properly making your financial plan is the start of your journey toward financial independence. Having a debt repayment strategy planned out is part of that plan and will help you feel less overwhelmed as you reach for your Big Financial Dream. The more steps you take toward financial freedom, the more empowered you'll feel, and the more your anxiety and stress will fade into oblivion.

- Speak to others who are going through or have faced divorce and debt and try to emulate their tactics.
- Seek professional help; nothing is more valuable than your mental and emotional health.
- Seek professional financial and debt-related counseling.
- Create a healthy schedule incorporating exercise, yoga, meditation, or other physical activities.
- Take your diet and sleep schedule seriously. Without these, your nerves will always be tightly strung.
- Make your financial plan properly; it will show you that there is a way to achieve financial independence.
- Plan your debt repayment strategy; you will feel less overwhelmed because you see a way out.
- Take the steps toward financial freedom; you will feel more empowered, and your anxiety and stress will fade into oblivion.

If you ever feel overwhelmed to the point of feeling suicidal, once again, here's who to contact.

National Suicide Prevention Lifeline: 1-800-273-TALK(8255)

Alternatively, you can call or text 988.

Your life is worth too much to those who matter for it to be thrown away. There is a way out, I promise.

Long-Term Financial Planning

Remember the financial plan I taught you to make in Chapter 3? In it, we discussed how your long-term financial planning should include debt repayment. Now's the time to put your debt repayment goals into your long-term financial plan so all your finances will be in one place.

Your debt repayment plan is essential to your financial plan because the faster you pay off your debt—especially the high-interest debt—the more your earnings will be available for other goals on your financial plan.

This works like the domino effect: you can pay off your debt to free up money for investments. Then, you will earn money from your investments for even more investments, retirement planning, insurance, a car, a house, and other necessities. Eventually, you will have enough to spend on whatever you want and be financially stable and free.

It all begins by paying off your debt.

Your planning stage is complete. Congratulations!

Celebrating Debt Payoff Milestones

Just like achieving your financial goals, paying off a debt is a massive accomplishment worth celebrating! It's impressive, and you should be proud of yourself!

Make the day you pay off a debt a day of celebration and gratitude for how far you've come. Feel free to do whatever makes *you* happy. Sleep in late and be lazy the whole day, or go out and picnic in the park with your kids. Give yourself a free pass to eat dessert or binge your favorite TV show; you've come so far!

Cross off the creditor you're now done with, and enjoy the strokes of your pen as they cross off that wretched name. Next, plan out what you'll do with the extra money. I encourage you to use the monthly payment from that debt you just paid off and add it to the monthly payment for the next creditor on your payoff list. After all, you're already used to that money being used for monthly debt reduction. Think about how fast you will get your debts paid off if you do that every time you pay off a creditor. Look at the next name on the list, and imagine yourself crossing that out, too, and then the next, until you're completely free, and you can use that money wherever you want. Each milestone brings you one step closer to that much-awaited, glorious day when you will experience debt freedom.

Today is a beautiful day. You're having a wonderful life and you are further away from your broken, newly divorced self than ever. You're healing and growing, and each milestone is proof of that.

Chapter Exercises and Reflections

A debt repayment journey is highly subjective and personal. It is incredibly challenging, and there are multitudes of options available. You need to choose the plan that works for YOU.

Many of the sections in this book offer options. That's a good thing because there is one perfect path that's tailor-made for you. However, deciding on the best path for you can be challenging.

Here are a few questions to help you at each step.

Assessing and Categorizing Debt

- *"What sorts of loans have I taken out?"*
- *"Are any of my payments overdue?"*
- *"What credit cards do I have in my name?"*
- *"Wait... is there collateral with this payment? Is that why the interest rate is suspiciously low?"*
- *"What terms did I agree to when I took this loan? Was I desperate?'*
- *Is this loan high-interest?"*

Spend some time mulling over each of these questions. Each time you come up with an answer, document it in your accounting plan.

Choosing a Repayment Strategy—Snowball, Avalanche, and Consolidation

- *"How bad is my emotional state? Do I go on impulse shopping sprees?"*
- *"Do I lose motivation quickly?"*
- *"How quickly do I need to see results to believe this will work? Do I tend to need instant gratification?"*
- *"Do I need to celebrate things, or is it enough to know I'm doing the right thing?*
- *"How good am I at keeping track of different appointments and dates?"*

If you answered yes to the first three, you'll likely want to use the snowball method, which will give you quick results and maintain motivation.

If you said yes to the fourth, you'll likely want to use the avalanche method. This method is for consistent people who don't need frequent celebrations to stay motivated.

Let me reiterate: it's okay to be a snowball because maintaining consistency is what matters.

Negotiation Versus Professional Help

- *"Am I brave? Am I confident enough to understand what I'm doing to take this on myself?"*
- *"Will I procrastinate and mess this up if I don't have a professional to guide or do it for me?*
- *"How much am I willing to pay a professional?"*
- *"How much help do I need to get started on this debt repayment plan?"*
- *"How much of it can I do independently with the help of family, friends, books, and articles?"*

The answers to these questions will help guide you independently.

Ask yourself all of these questions and more. You know your habits, and this is a long-term process that requires consistency. If you must sacrifice efficiency, it's a worthy exchange. Just keep fighting.

I wish you the very best of luck at the beginning of this phase of your journey! I'm proud of you!

Chapter 6:

Thriving in Your Finances: Managing Day-to-Day Expenses

"After my first divorce, I needed a new place to live with my kiddos and dogs. There was a house just down the road with a For Sale sign in the front yard, listed by the realtor I had used for years (and a very close friend). This was in 2009, and we were in the thick of the roughest housing market I'd known during my lifetime.

I picked up the phone and called my realtor friend, knowing full well that, following my bankruptcy, there was no way I would get a mortgage. I asked if he would find out if the sellers would be interested in renting to me with an option to buy down the road. I gave him permission to share my story with the sellers, as well as my history of owning my own home for years.

I didn't have a hope in you-know-where of my offer even being considered, let alone accepted. Imagine my surprise when my realtor called to let me know they were thrilled with the idea. Working in my favor was that I had been a homeowner for years, and they knew I would take care of the place as if it were my own and that they would receive rental income during the period before I could purchase.

The story's moral is not to give up all hope of reducing expenses. My rent for those first three years was much lower than a mortgage payment, and I had a four-bedroom house with a huge yard to call "home" with my kids."

We have already touched on some crucial financial decisions you must face after divorce. Now, it's time to move on to your everyday life, which has undoubtedly changed now that you have gone through all the legal proceedings and emotional turmoil.

The next crucial part is managing your monthly expenses without breaking the bank. Let's face it: your day-to-day life and budgeting would be easier if you had a partner. Your partner would help share the burden of everyday chores and expenses, and you'd have someone you know you could rely on. But now that you are independent again, navigating your finances, keeping the kids fed, and ensuring the dog gets walked feels like juggling five eggs simultaneously.

This chapter will explore the details of managing your daily expenses. We will analyze how to prioritize your essential expenses and create a tracking system to make navigating your expenses easier than ever. I will also offer some tips to make life easier for you, even easier than when you were married.

Prioritizing Essential Expenses

Things change rapidly after divorce. Now you are not just living alone; your entire lifestyle and way of managing cash have also changed. Transitioning from financial couplehood to single status can take time, and you must exercise patience. Remember always to be kind to yourself.

Before your divorce, you may have had a lifestyle that allowed for hired help or the ability to stay home with your kids. That might not be the case anymore. Now, it is likely that you will need to trim your budget, and you may need to reallocate the money you formerly set aside to go on vacation for things like school clothes and utility bills.

This can make you feel like you have lost all the good in your life, but remember that this is just a bump in the road. It's not the end of the line.

As we've done throughout this book, the first thing to do is assess your current financial situation and understand your finances are no longer the same. You may be dealing with a reduced income, new expenses such as alimony or child support, and even costs associated with setting up a new home.

In times like this, you need to prioritize the most essential expenses in your day-to-day life and cut costs from leisure spending, as much as you might not want to. Here are some main expenses you need to prioritize (Hurley, 2022).

1. Housing Stability

First and foremost, prioritize your rent or any mortgage payments and set that money aside every month to ensure a stable living environment for you and your children. You may need to reevaluate your current housing situation to determine if you can still afford the house you live in.

Downsizing is a great option, especially in the first few months or years after the divorce. Finding alternative affordable housing arrangements, living with some family members, or taking on roommates is also a good idea (Hurley, 2022).

2. Childcare Expenses

After ensuring you will have a roof over your head, your next most significant priority is your children. You will quickly realize that childcare these days is way more expensive than you might think, and I don't just mean someone to watch your young kids while you are at work. As a single mother, you must have enough money to pay for your kids' school and other extracurriculars, and have you noticed how fast they grow out of their clothes?

3. Food and Groceries

Another important priority is providing nutritious meals for you and your children. Plan your meals beforehand and create a grocery list. Not only does this benefit your budget, but it also eliminates having to make dinner decisions at the end of the day when you are tired and tempted to order take-out. Now that many grocery stores offer delivery or pickup, I have found it a great way to stick to my list as I'm not tempted by all the "extras" in the store that I don't need, not to mention the time I save not walking through all the store aisles.

If you struggle to budget your meals with your income, seek out local food assistance programs or community resources that provide support and groceries.

4. Basic Utilities

You must ensure your essential utilities—water, electricity, heating, and so on—are all covered in your budget. If it's hard to fit them all in, you can explore ways to reduce these costs with energy-saving practices or by checking out assistance programs for low-income families.

5. Healthcare Expenses

It is always essential to invest in good healthcare insurance. Affordable plans can be found through government programs or employer benefits (Hallberg, 2023).

6. One-Time Expenses

One thing nobody tells you about life after divorce is the one-time bills you will have to pay. In the months immediately following the divorce, be prepared to pay off several one-time bills, such as legal fees, down payments on a new home or rental property, and deposits to set up new utility services in your name.

Creating a System for Tracking Daily Expenses

Understanding your finances is one thing, but implementing your plan is quite another. I don't mean to scare you, but keeping track of your expenses can be challenging. Things can happen so rapidly that you won't even remember where you've spent your money.

Now is the time to take advantage of the advanced technology of tracking apps, which will make your life much easier. These tools have many clever yet easy-to-use features you can use right in the palm of your hand. There's an app out there for you, whether you like saving money in envelopes or working with figures and colored charts.

Here are some apps to check out, but always remember that apps come and go, so do some of your own research before you commit to one.

1. Rocket Money

Rocket Money is a popular replacement for the now-defunct Mint budgeting app. Rocket Money helps you build custom budgets and track your credit score and net worth while syncing with your bank and investment accounts. One of the best features of this app is the ability to sniff out and cancel subscriptions you no longer want or need. The free version is limited, so consider the Premium version for budgeting and subscription canceling.

2. Pocketbook

A great free app to consider is Pocketbook. This app helps you organize your finances by syncing your bank accounts and tracking your spending habits in real-time. It makes figuring out where you are spending your money easy and can help you see where to cut costs and avoid impulsive spending. It will motivate you to start saving by giving you the option of setting a safe spending limit or maximum weekly or daily spending amounts.

This app does come with some drawbacks. Most users complain that it takes a while to set up their accounts and that there are sync issues. Another thing to remember about this app is that you can only add accounts for banks on its list, so if you use a lesser-known bank, there might be better options.

3. Every Dollar (Formerly Mvelopes)

This app is Dave Ramsey's budgeting system. Based on the Zero Budget plan, you will love Every Dollar if you enjoy this system. This is yet another free app that allows you to connect accounts, including bank accounts and credit cards.

As is common with other apps, the free version is limited, but I recommend the Premium version here. This app also offers financial coaching with the paid version.

Numerous other budgeting apps are available. Make a list of your top priorities and then research which meets most of your criteria.

Negotiating Monthly Bills and Expenses

Once you've organized your expenses, it's time to take the next step: save.

The first rule of saving is that your needs must align with your income. Saving can only occur once you earn enough to fulfill your needs. If your expenses outpace your income, you cannot save the money you need to reach your dream. With that in mind, let's explore where you can reduce expenses.

If you know how to do it correctly, you can always negotiate your monthly bills and expenses with the service companies. Trimming your cell phone, internet, and cable bills is easiest and a great place to start.

Knowledge and information are your most essential tools when pursuing this negotiation option. First, look up the prices at each company you patronize and list what they offer compared to what you pay. Next, do the same with their competitors. You may find you are paying for services you don't even use. Perhaps the NFL package is no longer necessary in your house, or you can cut back by having your trash and recycling picked up twice a month instead of weekly.

Competitors' prices will be your best bargaining chip when negotiating with your service providers. Remain firm when negotiating; don't be afraid to switch providers if it's in your best interest. Also, remember to ask if any new promotions are going on. Cell phone companies are notorious for changing their plan pricing, and you may be paying more for less service without even knowing it!

Ask open-ended questions like, *"What can I do to lower my monthly bill?* What options do you have for me?"

Remember, small things can make all the difference for your budget (Quinlan, 2023).

Building a Cash Cushion

An emergency fund is one of the most intelligent money moves you can make. Nothing is better than having one available if needed (and no, that Prada bag you've always wanted is not an emergency).

Creating a cash cushion is a great way to support yourself financially against unforeseen long-term economic crises. Put away as much cash as you can as quickly as possible, even if it means pausing your debt payment method and only making minimum payments to pay your bills and attorney. Your emergency fund should have at least six months of funds saved so you can easily rely on it in emergencies.

You have no idea how unpredictable your life can be once you are alone. As disheartening as it is, you must remember you no longer have anyone to rely upon. You are your only support, and you'll have to deal with every obstacle alone. Once you acknowledge your situation and how easily things can go downhill, you will see that creating a cash cushion is the best thing you can do for yourself ("5 Ways to Improve," 2023).

Doing this can be as simple as saving every chance you get. It might not seem like much, but you will realize how much you can save by keeping track of your change. When you receive extra money, throw it in your emergency fund—received a tax refund? Put it in the emergency fund. Got a raise? Add the extra to your emergency fund each month. A bonus? That's the perfect opportunity to add to your emergency fund. Remember, even though you may feel that putting your money away is giving up things you want, it's the same money you will spend one day for an unexpected appliance replacement expense or job cutback emergency.

Keep your emergency fund separate from your cash cushion. Your emergency fund is for emergencies, while your cash cushion is for unexpected price increases or surprise expenses, like a plumber's visit to unclog your toilet.

Smart Saving Techniques

No woman likes to hear the words' savings' and 'shopping' in the same sentence, but hey—you can always be thoughtful and intelligent about your purchases, which is precisely what I want to help you with.

Here is my number one tip: always carry cash.

If you go shopping with a credit card, there will always be some cute little top or fantastic boots that tempt you to hand over your card. But if you have a limited amount of cash in your purse, you'll never have the option of overspending, which, as sad as it is, is necessary during this time of your life.

Take a shopping list with you. It will save you time and money by helping you stay focused on what you need rather than roaming around and trying to remember what you need. It's super easy to buy things you don't need while searching for what you do need.

Remember that sales, discounts, and promo codes are your best friends when saving while shopping. Be sure to take full advantage of end-of-season and holiday sales whenever you can. Buying things out of season can be super inexpensive; the lesser the demand, the lower the price—don't forget that.

Another shopping technique is to buy store brands instead of name brands. Store and name-brand products are often from the same manufacturer, and you mostly pay extra for the brand name.

Last but not least, do not, and I repeat, do not shop online until you get your finances under control. Going to a store to shop requires effort and planning. Shopping online requires neither of these and if you shop online when bored, it's too easy to buy things you might not even need. It is like being in a restaurant when you are hungry and want to order everything, even though you know you can't eat more than a sandwich.

1. Transportation and Commuting Costs

It is crucial to drive a fuel-efficient vehicle no matter where you are in your life. A car getting 30 mpg can save $918 in gas costs annually compared to one that gets 20 mpg. If you are open to considering other options, carpooling, public transportation, walking, or biking always exist. Many carpooling options will make things easier for you (Quinlan, 2023).

2. Entertainment and Leisure Activities

A 2020 survey showed that the average American spent $2,912 on entertainment that year alone ("13 ways," 2024). We don't need to spend that much, even if it is on average.

Who said you can't have fun on a budget? Your pockets may be tight now, but that will be the case only for a while. Enjoy the simple things like a picnic with your kids or a free community movie night at the park. Remain positive as you head toward a better future, and teach your kids you don't have to spend money to have a great time.

- ***Adventures in the Great Outdoors***

The outdoors can hold a variety of activities for you to try out. Picnics are an obvious fan favorite, but you can also go out swimming or hiking. Look into low-cost group activities you can enjoy alone or with your kids for a weekend out of the house. The great outdoors will boost your mood, help you reconnect with nature, and forget about your troubles for a while. Emma Healey, the founder of a money-saving blog for mothers, has an interesting tactic of searching for green spots in the neighborhood and discovering new nature spots with her children ("13 Ways," 2024).

- ***A Day at the At-Home Spa***

You don't need to go to the spa to feel beautiful. You may be surprised at how many homemade recipes and remedies help heal your skin and hair. Enjoy a peaceful time by celebrating yourself and releasing the day's stressors with a well-deserved do-it-yourself spa day at home. Check out YouTube and social media for some great ideas to pamper yourself.

- ***Entertaining Visits***

Books can open your mind to a world of wonder and magic. Utilizing your library and the Libby app gives you access to the world in book form. You can also sign up for a service like BookBub, where you receive daily emails with free and discounted books to download to your Kindle. Of course, you can always visit your local library and lose yourself amongst the stacks.

For fun outings, you can also look into discounted or free visits to zoos and museums. Walking around the city can help you discover new areas to visit. Try going to the local farmer's market, window shopping at the mall, or looking for hidden gems at the thrift store. Upcycling thrift store finds can make for exciting new craft projects.

- ***Creative Outlets***

Speaking of craft projects, why not take this opportunity to start a new art project or hobby? If you don't like how the table in the corner looks, paint it a different color or use recycled materials to make one you like better. You know what I'm talking about. They're the things that have been showing up on social media a lot lately, especially since COVID-19 hit. Who's to say you couldn't pull off something like that?

If these projects seem like too big of a step for you, why not design your own beaded jewelry or write that book you've always wanted to write? Writing is an excellent habit to adopt, not to mention an outlet for self-expression. Same with drawing, painting, sewing, etc. Take this time to stretch your wings and try new things. Who knows? Maybe your new hobby will turn into a nice little profit-making side hustle!

- ***Cooking and Baking***

Experiment with recipes and research different foods you might like to try. There are a ton of inexpensive recipes online, and many have videos that walk you step-by-step through the process. How about hosting a challenge with family or friends where you all make your recipe rendition and then rate which one tastes best? A potluck is also an inexpensive and fun way to get together while trying new dishes and enjoying some time to reconnect.

- ***Household Organizing***

Go around the house and get things organized and in order. Not only is it frustrating to be unable to find things when you need them, but it often forces you to buy things you already have but can't seem to find.

Are there things in storage that need sorting or thinning? You could hold a garage sale or go browsing at one held in your neighborhood to see if you can get any deals (Akingbade, 2015).

There are so many simple outlets that will be a source of comfort and entertainment to you during your post-divorce journey.

Research your interests and find something that fits with who you are and will entertain you the most.

3. Consider Downsizing Your Living Situation

We are all aware of the American dream of owning a house in the suburbs, but is owning a home really all that? One might argue that renting is more manageable than owning because that way, you won't be tied down with all of the responsibility of the investment. Keeping a house in good working order can be exhausting and expensive!

- ***Renting a Home***

Renting means knowing how much you'll pay for your monthly living accommodations. You also have the freedom to leave once your lease is up. The downside is that your rent may vary according to the area and could increase when your lease is renewed. Another downside is that you may be forced to leave if your landlord plans to sell the property.

- ***Owning Your Home***

Even though owning your home means you have the creative ability to change it and decorate it as you see fit, it can come with high maintenance costs. Depending on where you live, you may see considerable gains in equity, or you may have trouble selling your house for the amount you'd like due to fluctuations in the market.

Your choice between renting and owning depends on your financial goals and current budget. Research your situation's pros and cons before making a level-headed decision (Majaski, 2024).

Emergency Preparedness and Contingency Planning

The above suggestions can help you start contributing to your emergency savings fund. This accumulation, as a result of all of your careful budget cuts and savings, can help save your butt in a time of actual crisis. Who knows what lies in the future? I don't want to seem all doom and gloom, but you must be prepared for any contingency. It's not out of the realm of possibility to face medical emergencies, natural disasters, family problems, the high cost of tuition, and debt deadlines. You could find yourself in these situations that would decimate your financial stability if you don't have a safety net to back you up.

As we've discussed, being prepared releases the weight of the stress you carry on your shoulders. It also helps to bolster your mood and lead a healthier lifestyle, knowing one thing can't completely derail you financially.

Remember to replenish these funds if you must use them and review them regularly to check your status.

Seeking Community Resources and Support

Know that you aren't alone in this. Speak out. Ask family and friends for aid and support if needed, and look into local aid services in your area for assistance. Search for divorce support groups in your area, non-profit government organizations (NGOs) providing aid, and even religious organizations offering relief (Reseburg, 2024).

Community action agencies and government programs offer aid for those in a tight spot, and there is no shame in admitting you need a bit of help to get by until you can stand on your feet again.

Never think that this means you are incapable of surviving on your own. Think of reaching out as a temporary solution until the world returns to your favor again. Once you get your bearings, the world will open many avenues of opportunity for you to explore. Take the first step to ask for help and accept the aid provided with gratitude; you might be asked to return the generosity one day in kind.

These habits may seem tedious, but daily financial fixes can prove extremely fruitful in the long run. Things won't magically change unless you make the first move. The world will help you if you try to help yourself.

So far, you have learned about tracking your goals, reducing your debt, and minimizing your expenses. By now, you should have ample information on how to take a proactive approach in your daily life to keep moving forward.

Chapter 7:

Empowering Your Financial Future: Strategies for Maximizing Income

"At the time my emotional and financial world dropped out from under my feet, I'd just started an equine-assisted coaching business. Although I was working hard, it was a new modality that a lot of people just didn't understand, and if you think trying to explain life coaching to someone is difficult, try explaining horse-assisted life coaching!

I decided that a second certification in the life coaching field with a highly recognized coaching school would help me develop my program and improve my coaching skills. During the certification, I learned additional ways to coach and supplement the program I was currently building. (Not to mention, I would be a double-certified coach).

Just before beginning my coaching certification course, COVID hit. In-person coaching with the horses ground to a gut-wrenching stop. The good news was that I had plenty of time to take my online certification course and practice my new techniques with all my colleagues.

As the world started reopening, I decided to ramp up my side hustle of teaching western horse riding lessons to add some extra income. My lesson program filled to capacity quickly as parents sought ways to get their kiddos out of the house with limited exposure to large groups of other children. I discovered I enjoyed the lesson program so much that I chose not to pursue additional coaching clients in favor of teaching kids to ride, love, and care for horses."

It is said that a penny saved is a penny earned, but what happens when you can't save anymore?

- *"Where do I draw the line in sacrificing to save?"*
- *"I feel like a failure. I can't save any more."*
- *"What if I want to earn more pennies instead of saving them?"*

It's all right to draw a line in the sand if you feel deeper saving jeopardizes your health or self-esteem. What is essential, however, is that you are aware that your income has likely plummeted after your divorce. You're the one responsible for your money matters, so if you have yet to make significant adjustments to your standard of living, you may be living well beyond your means.

We've discussed saving money and spending money. Now, let's talk about earning money. This chapter is devoted to how you can earn more so that, between saving and cutting expenses and bringing in more income, you can set aside some money for investing or paying off debt faster. Here's to earning more!

Assessing Current Skills and Marketability

It's easy to convince yourself you need to be qualified or more experienced to land a job. After all, you are just a stay-at-home mom. What??? Are you out of your ever-loving mind? Underqualified? Inexperienced? Hardly! Don't sell yourself short. Being a stay-at-home mom is one of the most grueling jobs on the face of this earth.

Let's list just a few of the skills and qualifications your experience as a stay-at-home mom can offer a new employer.

- **Time Management:** You do this every day when you figure out how to get all the chores and errands done before dinner, get one kid to tutoring and the other to soccer practice, schedule the dog's checkup, and squeeze in a call to your mom.
    - On your resume, let's list this as: Experienced at balancing multiple tasks and responsibilities within a structured schedule.
- **Organization Skills:** If you think you aren't organized being a stay-at-home mom, think again! You must be organized to manage your budgets and bills, juggle the after-school calendar, and ensure the kids are walking the dog and taking out the trash. You organize more things by 8 a.m. than most people organize all day.
    - On your resume, let's list these talents this way: Efficiently manage budgets, schedules, and resources daily.

Get the picture? Here are a few other skills you can easily list on your resume that are sought after by employers for administrative positions, customer service, sales, project management, event planning, etc. Just add your own twist to how you describe it on your resume, as we did above.

- Problem-Solving
- Interpersonal Skills
- Negotiation
- Event Planning
- Project Management
- Financial Management
- Logistics and Coordination
- Household Administration
- Creativity

- Flexibility
- Attention to detail
- Childcare
- Cooking and Nutrition
- Effective Communication Skills

Also, list any talents or passions along with your qualifications. There may be a hidden gem you didn't realize was a marketable talent. Love kids? You could offer in-home childcare or after-school care. Do you love to teach? How about tutoring or being hired on as a teacher's aide? Do you love to write? There are a ton of opportunities out there as freelance writers and editors.

What is your skill or talent? What is your level of expertise in a particular field? What makes you special or unique? Please write it down, believe in your gifts, and work on improving them as you look for related jobs or business opportunities.

Exploring Career Advancement Opportunities

Now that you've listed your talents, passions, and skills, let's look at your certifications in a field you'd like to pursue.

What if the only proof you have of your skill is the results you produce? Is there a way to prove you're a good baker without taking samples to all potential customers or employers? Let's take a closer look.

Compare these two statements.

- *"I'm a good baker because I've been baking divine pastries, bread, and cakes for the past ten years."*
- *"As an XYZ Culinary Institute graduate, my baked goods speak for themselves."*

Which one sounds better? Professional certification gives you an edge over years of experience because our culture has been trained to believe that institutes and education are trustworthy. In contrast, those pastries and bread may be "divine" only to your family.

You only gain credibility once there is enough word-of-mouth in your favor, and at this point, you are newly divorced and struggling to find your feet. Earning the certificates will vouch for you as you look for a job.

Knowing how to negotiate a pay raise might be helpful if you are already established and happy in your current job.

- Know that your company would gladly give you a promotion if you can prove you can fill an available, higher-paid opening instead of hiring and training a new person. It will save them time and effort if they hire you instead. Knowing this should help boost your confidence.
- Know your market value. There are many online platforms where you can find an estimate of the market value for the role you want to fill. Once you have completed this research, only settle for what you're worth.
- Emphasize your value. If your employer feels you can fill a role but need to be more qualified, they might offer you the promotion without a raise. Be on the lookout for this, know your worth, and fight for fair compensation. Prove you're invaluable to the company and back up your argument with numbers, percentages, and reviews from your clients and superiors. Understand the additional workload you'll be taking on, and don't settle for less.
- If your employer cannot offer you a significant pay raise, there are other things for which you can negotiate. For example, if you get to work from home twice a week, you could use those days to catch up with your household management, something you now have to juggle alongside your job. You could also ask for company-sponsored education or training that will help you in the future. In short, alongside your raise in pay, look for other options that will help you attain pay raises in the future.
- Ask your supervisor or boss which skills you need to qualify for a raise or how long you could expect to wait for the

company to give you one. Set a date for a meeting to revisit the situation and discuss it further. Remember that communication is critical in a negotiation. Book the date for your meeting, go in with your head held up high, and re-negotiate.

- Be sure to retain your employers' goodwill at all costs. Understand their answers and look for other options to meet your needs and achieve your goals, apart from more earnings.

For example, if you have a job in graphic design and recently earned a certification in photography, now is the ideal time to apply for a promotion or salary raise. Show your employer what you've learned and how it will add value to your workplace performance.

Pursuing Additional Education or Training

Let's review ways to earn certifications, including additional learning to improve skills.

Online Courses

One of the cool things about being post-COVID is that almost every college and university offers online courses. You can get degrees and certifications directly from Harvard, Yale, or other universities from the comfort of your home. These degrees are certified and less expensive than you might think, and you can often complete them whenever you have some free time, allowing you to earn certificates and degrees without taking time off your current job.

You can also check out sites such as Coursera.org and edX.org to explore classes that can enhance your skills and career or even launch you in a new direction in a higher-paying field.

In-person Courses

Although it may be tough to attend in-person university classes if you have children at home or are currently working, many universities and colleges offer evening and weekend in-person courses. Look up schools near you and inquire about degrees or certifications in your field if this is your preferred route.

Apprenticeship/Mentor

An apprenticeship or mentorship with a professional in your field will go a long way in developing your skills and moving you forward in your career. For example, working with, or taking classes with, a highly regarded chef proves that you're good at your job because you were taught by the best. This mentorship can also help expand your network when seeking a new career or advancement opportunity.

If this interests you, visit the websites of famous artists, bloggers, videographers, photographers, bakers, etc., as many will post online or in-person learning opportunities. Invest in these classes if your budget allows it. Learning a skill is an excellent investment because it increases your worth in the employment market. It also provides a solid foundation for your new startup or job placement by proving you're worthy of the position.

In short, if you have a unique skill or talent, you must translate it into a language people respect, understand, and trust. Not only will certifications and 'professional' training guide you on how to use your talent, but they will also provide the trust and confidence of the people to whom you are marketing your skills.

Considering Career Changes

What do you do if your current job isn't giving you room for growth or the opportunity to earn as much as you need to cover your expenses? How might you switch to something more lucrative? Should you even make the switch? Good questions. Let's look into it a bit more.

You can change your career path or pursue a different role if your previous one didn't allow for enough growth or contentment, especially if you took it up when you were desperate. According to

LabourIQ, "salaries for new hires are about 7% higher on average than the median pay for people who already have similar roles" (Taylor & Lebowitz, 2023). Why not become someone else's new hire?

The ball is in your court when a new company offers you a job. Companies may offer very lucrative pay and benefits packages if you've done your research, know how to market your skills, and have attained your certifications or required degrees. Now is the time to negotiate with prospective or current employers. Remember, your company prefers to give you a promotion if you prove you can fill a spot instead of hiring and training a new person, so you should ask for higher pay and benefits if you are considering staying. The bottom line is you can choose between multiple options before deciding to stay at your current job or leave for greener pastures.

To know if you should switch jobs at all, ask yourself

- *"Is my current job suited to my skills?"*
- *"Do I enjoy what I'm doing?"*
- *"Am I earning as much as I need to?"*
- *"Do they intend to pay me more eventually?"*
- *"Am I dying inside here?"*

How you answer these questions will help you decide whether you want to continue or move to another company. Sure, perhaps you will earn more at a new job, but do you want to deal with the turbulence of that shift? Have your current colleagues supported you through the rough phases of your divorce? Does your boss give you the flexibility you need when you're overwhelmed? Is it worth the risk to look for a new job now? Ask yourself why you want to leave; you'll know what to do when you know your answer.

Considering Entrepreneurship

Consider entrepreneurship when switching career paths. If your dream has always been to own a business, your current job can provide security and financing while you get your dream up and running.

Does it sound scary? Sure it does. But consider all the benefits of owning your own business, such as setting your own schedule, staying home with your kiddos, or providing a service or product you've always wanted to deliver. At the same time, consider all the pitfalls you may encounter, like taking a while to make money, working with employees, all the inner workings of owning a business, and how much your business will tie you down. I recommend talking to other business owners and working with a coach to ensure you get your business set up correctly and start on the path to profitability from the beginning. You are not alone in entrepreneurship, so take advantage of those who have forged the path before you.

Owning a business does not necessarily mean having a physical brick-and-mortar shop. You can run many business opportunities from home, utilizing your accumulated skills and talents. Start selling your skills if you think they're good enough to be sold to the public. Properly marketed, your skills will sell and make you money.

Starting a business can feel slow and tedious as you gain momentum and build your reputation. If you choose to stay in your current job while you start your business, you can balance your business's workload as you transition slowly, using your job as a safety net until you're ready to spread your wings and fly.

A business is like a child you raise and nurture, investing time, effort, heart, and soul. It's a gratifying experience, but there will be long hours as you work on your product (whether physical or intellectual), design marketing strategies and materials, set up your books and financing, and all the general overall day-to-day tasks necessary to succeed. Every step will be stressful, but since when was it easy to raise a child?

If you're up for the challenge, entrepreneurship can be extremely rewarding. There's nothing better than working at something you created, own, and love. You're the boss, and you call the shots. True, the initial phases can be an uphill battle, but if you're passionate about it, you'll thrive. The hardest part is showing up and believing in yourself. Speaking from experience, it's worth every sleepless night and long day.

Leveraging Side Hustles and Freelance Opportunities

What happens if you need help keeping up your income while starting your business? What if your job needs to pay you more, but switching jobs or career paths isn't an option? Allow me to introduce you to the world of freelancing and side hustles.

A **side hustle** is where you make extra money by doing small jobs for others. Simple ones include

- babysitting
- dog walking
- blogging
- content writing
- providing tech support online
- photography
- providing small-scale, healthy cooking
- accompanying an elderly person
- tutoring at any level
- any service you can offer for small payments

These short-term jobs can be quite lucrative. The best part is that you don't need stressful interviews or required qualifications; everybody is qualified.

Freelancing is being self-employed while working professionally for clients, including companies. If you're a freelance web designer, a good example would be designing a page for a blogger or a startup. You can freelance as a side hustle or take it on as your full-time job.

If you're interested in freelancing, you can quickly learn the necessary skills. As discussed, go to *Udemy*, *Coursera*, or *EdX* and pick a course to train you for your desired job. With freelancing, you can learn on the go while adding contracts to your resume.

Focus on your accreditation and experience when writing your freelancing resume. Make your resume public so freelancing opportunities can find you while you are also searching for gigs. However, do not ever leave your freelance job search only to the whims of algorithms and the chance that clients will find you. It's best to proactively put your resume in front of the people looking for your skills and talents.

An excellent place to start your freelancing career is to try platforms like Fiverr and Upwork. Although these markets can be tricky because you need a good client history to get consistent work, if you can be patient and effectively market your skills and talents, these platforms act as middlemen to showcase your availability. The client pays the platform before asking you to do the work. Once the job is done, the platform pays you. This way, you are assured of payment and avoid any scams. The cons? They'll take up to 20% of your pay.

Alternatively, you could try online options posted on platforms such as Indeed and LinkedIn. These sites connect you directly to the client so you can negotiate with them. The plus is that you get to keep what you earn. The negative, however, is that the client could easily ask to see your work, plagiarize it, and not pay you. I highly recommend you speak to an attorney to determine how to write an employment contract to best protect your interests. Always take steps to protect yourself and your work.

It's also good to check the clients' reviews before applying for jobs. It's horrible when you're hard-pressed, hopeful, and working hard on a project, but when it's time to get paid, the client ghosts you. You'll wind up spending the next month begging them to pay you, but they've vanished, taking your motivation with them. Have you ever been in such a position? If you haven't, let me assure you that it's a pathetic way for a client to act. Never apply for a freelance job before ensuring the client has good reviews. It's just not worth the risk.

Another option to supplement your income is **online teaching or tutoring**. Again, choose a platform with a middleman system so you won't get scammed. You'll need some certification to teach in the US, but online teaching can be quite lucrative once you have it. Simply Google 'online teaching' jobs or 'teaching online.' You may be surprised at the opportunities available for full-time or part-time teachers.

With side hustles and freelancing, the best part is the exposure to a whole new world of opportunities. You might start doing a few different jobs on the side, and as you discover your passion for one of them, decide to pursue that area and build your reputation. Before you know it, you can slowly wean off your full-time job. Alternatively, you could keep your job while supplementing your income with other options, not because you need it, but because you enjoy the work. A job can be pretty fun if you're not dependent on it, especially when you don't need them, but they need you. Use your side hustles to get you to that point.

Navigating Part-Time or Flexible Work Arrangements

Suppose you choose to take up a side hustle, freelancing, or start your own business, and it's going well and growing, but you want to keep your job to alleviate financial stress or supplement your income. At this point, you may want a flexible, part-time job to allow you to continue on your entrepreneurial path. It's time to conduct another round of negotiations with your current employer or apply for a different job to establish a better schedule that suits your needs.

Setting Your Priorities

Sit down and make a list of priorities so you are clear on what you want and need in your job. Of course, you want to stay off the streets, and you need food on the table, decent clothes, and utilities, but beyond that, is money the only thing you need?

You've worked on sorting through your emotions. You must also understand your body's physical and emotional limits and be kind to yourself. If you have dependent children, you must also factor them into your equation and ensure you have the time to care for them and raise your family. After all, just as you've lost your support and partner, their relationship with their parents has been affected. You must be there to support them, acknowledge their feelings, and alleviate their insecurities during a highly emotional time.

Once you have your priorities straightened out—and take your time doing this—let your prospective or present employer know about them. You'll have to be firm at this point and present your dealbreakers, such as long hours or travel. Know that many other jobs and opportunities will be able to accommodate your needs.

Now, it's time to find the perfect part-time or flexible arrangement job that works with your family.

An example might be a school-associated job, such as teaching or administrative work. These are generally designed around a child's schedule. Just be sure the school you work in has roughly the same schedule as where your kids attend. You don't want to discover your spring break is an entirely different week from your kids and find yourself scrambling to find child care.

If you're in a different field, there are generally opportunities to work part-time.

Indeed and Zip Recruiter are excellent platforms to search for part-time work. As you browse the listings for opportunities, note any certifications and qualifications you may need to land your ideal job. This is the perfect time to nail down any education you may lack.

To further explore part-time options, fit side hustles and freelancing options into your schedule. The best part about these options is you decide how you spend your time and which projects you want to work on. That is not to say that you should stay home and shirk your money-earning responsibilities; choose this option only if you have the discipline to keep searching for freelance opportunities as they fit into your schedule.

Negotiating Compensation and Benefits

Have you ever seen that student at school who could convince his teachers to give extensions and re-tests as if they had a right to it? Or perhaps you've seen a child with the whole world wrapped around their pinky finger. How do they do it? How can you do it as an adult?

Children know exactly what they can ask for and what they can't. The average child won't ask for a million dollars, but they might ask for ice cream. They might ask for a tub and settle for a cone because you can give it to them. Both are within the child's expectations for ice cream.

What is your ice cream expectation? What do you expect to earn at your job? What perks and benefits do you want? What if you don't stop there but ask for a little more? Your employer might try to negotiate it down, but why not ask for that tub of ice cream, especially when asking for a cone might leave you with nothing more than a spoonful. List your skills and perceived value to the company beyond your current role and negotiate accordingly. Can you bring your loyalty, commitment, and effort into the game and ask for compensation?

Have you ever heard a child negotiate for something they want by providing something they believe you want? Does *"If I clean my room, can I go to the movie with my friends?"* or *"Can I get a puppy? I promise to feed it, clean up after it, and take it for a walk every day!"* sound familiar?

You could ask for the opportunity to prove yourself by meeting additional XYZ requirements in exchange for a bonus or the promise to take on extra work in return for a more significant pay raise.

Do children ever ask you to take them to the park or mall when you're in a huff and shouting at everyone and everything that crosses your path? Do they ask when you're mad at them, or do they wait until you've cooled down, or they've done something deserving a reward? Children are excellent judges of emotions. Similarly, you should be able to gauge your company's financial status and wait until they've made some profit or your boss is in an excellent mood so they'll be more likely to accept your proposal for a promotion. Time your moves wisely.

You can look for inspiration anywhere, and sometimes, it's good to look at how your kids might handle something and rediscover your inner child. Go back to a time when you knew what to do instinctively. Your child still lives within you, fearless and wise. Connect with your younger, innocent self and try to emulate her. You'll be able to unleash a confident, unscarred version of yourself who knows her way around negotiation and life to make the changes she wants to see. Go for that tub of ice cream!

Exploring Passive Income Streams

There are many options to help bring some more money into your household, but one of my favorites is **passive income.** Just as debt creeps up and devours your earnings, passive income flows in and adds to your spendable money without much effort.

What is this holy grail called passive income? Passive income is when you get regular earnings from sources other than contractors or employers. Although second jobs can provide more money, they need constant effort and stretch your time and energy resources. Passive income is where you invest your money or time upfront, and instead of a one-time payout, payments continue into the future.

Some examples include

- writing a book
- renting out property
- creating an online course on Udemy
- blogging or vlogging
- affiliate marketing on your blog or vlog
- selling photography
- dividend-giving stocks
- renting out a part of your house or parking space (Royal, 2024).

As you've probably guessed by now, passive income does not come without some risk. If you are writing a book or creating an online course, you can expect to invest lots of time in creating content or an online presence. If your content doesn't "blow up" or "go viral" immediately, it can feel like a complete waste of time. Similarly, with rental properties, there isn't much you can do if the tenants refuse to pay on time, you have trouble renting the property, or you need to foot some extensive repairs.

My point is not to encourage or discourage you from a specific money-making system. I'm trying to educate you on the pros and cons of each system and teach you, in the process, that there are risks in even the most harmless and seemingly lucrative ventures. You just need to know enough to be on the lookout for them and not automatically believe in schemes that seem win-win at first blush.

In my case, I started out after my first divorce with practically nothing in my hands. My passive income stream was rentals. The income continues flowing today as long as I maintain the properties and keep collecting the rent. How cool is that?

Avoiding Scams

Remember the mouse that died because he could never understand why the cheese was free? I've tried to teach you how to look for hidden risks in every situation. If something looks too good to be true, it probably is.

"Just fill out this personality form, and here's $2 for free!" is what a quiz from Cambridge University researcher Aleksandr Kogan's website advertised in 2010. All you had to do was give a tiny, fine-printed bit of access to your Facebook profile. In reality, this "personality quiz" was only designed to gain access to your and your friends' Facebook profiles to extract data somebody would use to manipulate elections. Ring a bell?

This was the infamous Cambridge Analytical Scandal, which compromised 50 million accounts because 270,000 people didn't know better than to accept free money ("Cambridge Analytica," 2022). See where this is going? If something is for free, look for the why, how, and where, and beware.

Whether it's an online job on LinkedIn or an MLM scheme that promises you money for marketing and then disappears (or anything similar), beware. Be especially cautious if you feel that rush of blood and excitement while thinking it's just the opportunity you've been waiting for.

Beware of people who will play on your desperation. Know that when you feel these intense emotions, someone is likely inciting them to override your better senses. A dead giveaway is when they put a timeframe or expiring clock on a once-in-a-lifetime opportunity that sounds too good to be true. There are a lot of these scams out there. Do your research and proceed cautiously in this age of digital warfare for your money and personal information.

Balancing Work and Personal Life

I touched upon this in the section where we spoke about negotiating part-time or flexible schedules, and I can't stress it enough. Divorce isn't the end of the world or a do-or-die situation where either you work the living daylights out of yourself, or you'll be out on the streets. Be kind to yourself and try to be efficient and hard-working instead of working hard.

We are often exposed to people who brag about how hard their schedules are and how little sleep they get in favor of working. People glorify all-nighters and unhealthy work-life balances, implying that sleeping less and having no free time for yourself equates to success. But is working groggily into the night worth it when you could get double the work done in the morning when your mind is fresh? What about after years of burning the candle at both ends, you have to spend the extra money you worked so hard to earn on medical exams and prescription meds? And what about your kids? They grow up fast and will leave the nest sooner than you think. Although you may feel your hard work is providing them with everything they want, in the end, they will remember the time you spent with them at the park or hanging out over the expensive shoes or fancy house.

You need to be reasonable and create a **work-life balance.** As we've discussed before, you need to have your priorities well-defined. Prioritize family first, alongside your mental, emotional, and physical well-being. The money will come later. If your employer cannot respect your boundaries, they will never appreciate or respect any of the work you do. Choose a job where you'll have *some* flexibility to take care of what's important and still manage to meet your work responsibilities because balance matters … whether that means negotiating terms with your boss or moving to a job with the flexibility to work from home twice a week, find what works best for you.

The bottom line is that spending and earning go hand in hand. You cannot expect to hang around at home and think that a minimum-wage or part-time job will make ends meet. It also doesn't mean working a 50-hour week is in your best financial and emotional interest.

To achieve balance in your life, you need to find the juncture between earning a healthy amount, saving a healthy amount, investing a healthy amount, and supplementing your earnings with passive income from investments and other side hustles while keeping an eye on your debts and expenses.

At every point, you'll have to negotiate terms that suit you better, avoid scams that could cripple your self-esteem and your pocketbook, and strike a chord that will work for you. It's all about finding your balance.

Trust me, the journey will become easier. As long as you stay true to your priorities, you will learn so much about yourself and what works for you. Everyone who has been through what we've experienced can relate to your struggles. They've found their feet, and you will, too, if you keep going!

Chapter Exercises and Reflections

Whew! That's a lot to digest, isn't it? We've learned about earning from everywhere possible while still focusing on savings and balancing work and family. Although it may sound complicated, you can do it! Let's look at the journey through questions you can ask yourself.

First off, it's about **knowing your worth and options.**

Ask yourself questions like

- *"What's my secret skill or talent?"*
- *"Do I experience joy and fulfillment in my current field of work?"*
- *"If I'm this talented at _______________, why do employers not notice my skills?"*
- *"How do I prove I'm worthy of the position or raise?"*
- *"How do I compete with other people's resumes?"*
- *"I have the skills—how do I market them correctly?"*

Let your answers to these questions guide you as you navigate through the first sections of this chapter.

Next, let's talk about this elusive thing called **balance.**

Ask yourself:

- *"Am I neglecting my kids/parents?"*
- *"Does my employer appreciate the effort I put into my job?"*
- *"Will get a raise anytime soon?"*
- *"How much more money do I need to hit the goals on this month's financial plan?"*
- *"What side hustles can I do to hit that goal without taking more time away from my family?"*
- *"Can I stop working now if I'm already hitting my financial plan goals?"*
- *"Can I find a passive income to supplement my wages without breaking the bank to get it started?"*

Let me assure you that you can chillax as long as you're hitting your financial goals and covering a little more. You've earned your night's sleep and family time, so enjoy it. Guilt will only make you feel worse until you snap and give up. Keep yourself from getting to that point.

Here's what not to worry about:

"Sally's best friend went through a divorce last year, and she's so far ahead of me in the game… I've heard she pulled all-night shifts at a restaurant as well as working at her day job until she got there. Why can't I do that?"

You're not Sally's best friend, so stop right there. Remember, everyone processes grief and divorce differently. Your body works differently, and there's no race here. Never compromise your health or family for money because you will never get those years of your youth with your kids again. No one said you're not allowed to enjoy the journey even when the going gets tough.

As for **negotiations**, I asked you to observe a child and see how they negotiate their way in life. Find your equivalent of this and act on it. It's always possible to draw on a child's confidence and intuition and use them to guide you in serious situations and deal with them confidently. Remember, you're still growing and learning. Just as a child is fine with falling, bursting into tears, accepting help and bandages, and healing, you must get up and give yourself time to recover. Soon, you will be able to proudly flaunt your emotional scars and bruises and show them off to other 'kids' your age, saying, "You know, I fell a few years ago and had a nasty bruise. It was yellow and blue and ran deep into my core, but I kept at it, and here I am! I survived, and I'm fine."

This point in life is worth fighting for.

Chapter 8:

Pay Yourself First: The Importance Of Saving And Maximizing Your Savings After Divorce

"My humiliation was genuine, and I felt I was as low on the financial chart as I could get when I discovered the rental agency that managed the house I was going to rent required my parents to co-sign my lease. BUT, at least I wasn't living with them, so there's that!

I knew beyond a shadow of a doubt that I would claw myself out of the financial hole I found myself in and own my home again, which meant saving as much money as I could each and every month. The best thing I ever did was ALWAYS set aside money in my savings account before spending on anything else. This enabled me to come up with a down payment for my house.

I played the game of talking myself out of a cup of coffee and instead immediately transferring the money I would spend directly into my savings account. I put every last cent of windfall money in my savings. I budgeted every month, and anything left over was transferred into my savings account, so every month, my checking account started out at zero.

I set up a savings account I could easily access for emergencies and a mutual fund investment account that was a little tougher to raid.

Although I now have multiple investment accounts, to this day, I still have that automatic $10/week deposit sent to my Acorns.com account, where it is invested on my behalf. "

Debt repayment under control. Check. Expenses reduced. Check. Income maximized. Check. Thanks to your advanced budgeting knowledge, your finances are balanced, and you are on track to repay your debt with your plan.

Until disaster strikes. The furnace in your home goes out. You can't live without heat, but your only option to get it fixed is to put it on your credit card, and that only adds to your debt and sets you back, once again, on your debt repayment plan. Sigh. This is NOT how you saw this month going.

What if you had another option to pay for the furnace? What if you had money in a savings account you could use for this setback without affecting your monthly budget or adding to your debt?

When we focus on how to live financially independent lives, savings and emergency funds are often overlooked.

The Importance of Saving Post-Divorce

It may not be something as big as replacing a furnace that throws a wrench into your budget plan. Often, it's as simple as fluctuating salaries, job changes, childcare, and domestic items getting more expensive that can set you back.

Saving up will help you construct a foundation for your future. With a separate portion of your income dedicated to your savings, you can make financial decisions more confidently, knowing that if things go south, you'll have a safety net to fall back on.

With your savings in good order, you'll be able to proceed with your financial plan and Big Dream and still have enough to handle any pitfalls that might come along the way. Saving will help you control your situation and prevent you from panicking and worrying.

Instead of, *"How the hell am I going to pay for the furnace to get fixed? I don't have enough to deal with that right now. What will I have to cut down on to pay for this?"* your thoughts might go something like this: *"Okay, I need to get a new furnace. I'm sure I have enough savings for that. If I cut down on my luxuries for a time, I'll be able to replace my savings and deal with the furnace."*

See the difference? Where one sounds panic-stricken and lost, the other sounds empowered and confident and has a set direction.

Savings also helps you collect funds for your long-term goals. It seems easy to talk about setting long-term goals, such as buying that new house, but when you get lost in the "now" of paying your bills and living your day-to-day life, your goals might slip from your mind. Then, when the opportunity comes for you to achieve it, you'll realize you need more money.

Savings allows you to work on your present while also building toward your future.

Creating a Savings Mindset

Putting money aside may seem easier said than done, and people in different financial situations may view "savings" differently. However, establishing a savings mindset and getting it done (no matter how large or small the amount) will give you control and confidence over your financial situation. It protects you from feeling insecure, vulnerable, and lost when faced with unforeseen circumstances.

Focusing on saving money and avoiding unnecessary spending is a positive and proactive way of thinking that enables you to make every financial decision with intention and a fixed direction rather than making choices based on luck and gut feelings.

How can you cultivate this new mindset? The first step is to gather some tips and tricks that will help change your spending habits and work more on saving.

Tips to Build Savings Habits

Write Savings Goals Down

Think about your savings goals and what you hope to achieve through them. Set a specific amount for which you want to see your savings grow each month. For others, it works better to forgo a monthly goal and set a particular amount you want to save by a specific time. Remember, this is a goal, so make sure it follows the SMART goal guidelines we discussed earlier. Writing down your goals turns them into commitments and compels you to stick with them. Put these goals somewhere you'll see them, such as on your closet doors, bedside wall, or table, and use them to spur your motivation for the day.

Find a Savings Buddy

If saving seems like a drag, why not find a friend to do it with? It's always good to keep connections with like-minded people, as these connections will lead to productive conversations that can help motivate you to reach your goal. It can be a friend, family member, coach, or anyone who can help you move forward and give you advice.

Automatc Savings Transfers

The easiest way to amass savings is to make small and frequent transfers from your checking account into your savings account before you even begin implementing your monthly budget. Acorns.com is an excellent tool that automatically invests as little as $5/week on your behalf. You will be amazed at how quickly that little amount will grow.

You can also utilize your bank's automatic transfer function to transfer a set amount into your bank savings account each week or month. Set it up once, and you won't have to worry about doing it again unless you want to adjust the amount transferred. Then, you can sit back and watch your savings grow.

Analyze Your Spending Motivation

As mentioned earlier, saving money can be difficult for some, but now is the time to understand why. Ask yourself:

- *"What makes me want to spend money?"*
- *"Do I need this? Is this purchase necessary?"*
- *"Can I wait to buy this later? Do I have to buy it now?"*

When we ask ourselves these questions, we slowly unravel the emotions connected to those sudden needs for splurging. Instead of spending willy-nilly, we want to convince ourselves to make decisions with planning and forethought, learn to analyze the situation, and then make the appropriate decision. This includes credit card spending. It's super easy to convince yourself that you "need" something when you can "just put it on the credit card." Remember, adding credit card debt only messes with your debt repayment plan.

Set Realistic Savings Goals

Sometimes, you can be too motivated and make far-fetched savings goals that only result in feeling bad about yourself when they aren't achieved as fast as you wish. Then, when you look back on those goals and your slow growth, you adopt a pessimistic mindset and wonder if you are moving forward at all. It's essential to set realistic goals. There is no harm in starting small. Starting small lets you celebrate an achieved goal and motivates you to set a new one with just a bit more stretch.

Find Purchase Alternatives

I will never tell you to avoid doing what you like because it interferes with your savings plan. However, if you continuously believe you deserve the new outfit, the fancy meal, or the designer bag, you'll always be withdrawing from your savings.

Now, let's consider some ways to discover cost-effective options that enable you to scratch your "fun" itch without derailing your savings plan. Instead of stopping for a fancy coffee on your way to work, what if you make your fancy coffee at home? There are tons of fun coffee recipes on the web that look amazing!

What if you host a potluck dinner with your friends instead of eating out at a restaurant and ask each guest to bring their "special recipe" item and copies of the recipe for anyone who might want it?

Instead of going out for lunch at work, team up with colleagues to do a "lunch swap." (I actually did this for years when I worked in the corporate world and LOVED it). Someone else's leftovers may be an incredible new meal to someone else. Again, have those recipes ready for anyone who might want to try their hand at making your dish for their family.

Make watching movies at home special by breaking out the special treats (that are only for movie nights). You can also set up a screen outside and host an outdoor movie night for your friends and family. Ask your guests to bring treats to share to add to the specialness.

Get the idea?

If you don't have cost-friendly options, adjust your budget by cutting back in another area. Your budget and savings plan are unique to you. Make them what they need to be to satisfy all your needs, both physical and emotional.

Stay Motivated: Check Your Balances

Set a day of the week to check your savings accounts to see your progress and to keep yourself motivated by the knowledge that your hard work is paying off for a better future. There will come a time when you won't have to worry about this anymore, and you're getting closer to it. Stay motivated and be determined to cement the habit of saving money in your mind.

Identify Short- and Long-term Savings Goals

Setting goals for the future is more important than you may realize, and setting savings goals is a big part of that plan. Goals provide a roadmap, a checklist, and a direction to follow as you advance along your financial journey. Only you know what you're moving toward, and hitting goals allows you to celebrate while also motivating you to continue.

Reaching any goal builds a sense of pride and provides a foundation as you create your future life. Reaching savings goals gives you and your kids much-needed stability and peace of mind. You will no longer be on a rocking piece of driftwood, seconds away from toppling into the violent waves. No. You will be on the ship you built for yourself, keeping your head above the water and nowhere close to drowning.

Some examples of short-term financial goals you might expect to attain include:

- changing your job
- building up an emergency fund
- repaying your debts

These are simple goals you can reach without requiring a lot of time to do them. Long-term goals, however, require significantly more time to reach. These might include:

- owning a house
- advancing your career
- going on a trip abroad (Griffiths, 2023)
- retirement

Regardless of the types of goals you set, you must make sure they are SMART goals, stay motivated, and stick to them while also understanding that you may have to adjust them if the situation calls for it. Going on that trip may take longer than planned, but if you stick to your savings plans, the trip may come sooner than you think.

As Tara Eisenhard says, "You can envision your new life any way you want. But what you want won't happen unless you commit to making it a reality. What goal will you set first?" (2016).

Budgeting for Savings

To adjust your budget to include savings as an obligation, you need to analyze your expenses and see where to cut down on unnecessary spending or find cost-effective alternatives.

If you have a limited budget, it might be hard to figure out how much you can allocate for savings. It doesn't matter what amount you start with; it matters that you start. Start with $25 a month, or $10, or $5. Put that amount in your savings account and pat yourself on the back that you did it. When you feel comfortable with your amount, try increasing it the next month. Again, this is your savings plan, so put away what you can afford, not what someone else thinks you can afford.

Another way to save is to dedicate a certain percentage of your income to savings. This may be easier if your income fluctuates from paycheck to paycheck. Again, you can choose any percentage you feel comfortable with ... 1%, 5%, 10%, or whatever you're comfortable with. Just start!

Next, set a savings goal and check your account frequently. Once you reach the goal, you can enjoy a small celebration and set a new goal. This will help you remain motivated ("Tips," n.d.).

Your savings plan is NOT a luxury; it is a necessity, and it's essential to include it as a line item in your budget. This is not a negotiable budget item, and it is imperative that you "pay yourself first" before spending on anything else. I don't care if you plan to pay yourself $1 or $1000; get that money in the account and then divide the rest into your budget items.

Maximizing Savings on a Limited Budget

I have clients who choose to forgo a coffee house drink on the way to work and immediately transfer the amount they would have spent on the coffee into their savings account. This can be a fun way to challenge yourself to cut back on things you want (but don't need) while still allowing you to buy that coffee that was already in your budget if you choose to.

Let's look at some other ways to contribute to your savings:

Cooking

Buy ingredients in bulk and discover new recipes to try out at home. Get the kiddos involved with the cooking and meal planning to have some great family time and teach them to cook, save money, and budget. Not only will you establish a fantastic and fun habit and teach your kids about money and budgets, but you just might enhance your cooking skills. Win/win in my book!

Save On Utilities

Challenge your kids to be more aware of the electricity and water possibly being wasted around the house. Make it a contest to see who can come up with the most ideas to cut back on electricity and water use. Some examples would be turning the bathroom faucet all the way off (no annoying drips to keep you awake at night), unplugging the coffee maker when it's not in use, shutting off lights when you're the last one to leave a room, and turning off the TV when nobody is watching.

Commute And Transportation

Transportation to work or for other travel can take a sizeable bite out of your budget. If you live somewhere with good, reliable public transit, consider saving the cost of a vehicle by opting for public transportation. Look into nearby bus routes to see if this option is feasible for you. What about walking or riding your bike to nearby places? (The cool thing about this option is the added health benefits, both physically and mentally).

Save On Housing Costs

Maintaining a house can be one of the most significant expenses you'll ever have. Consider renting an apartment or sharing a place with a roommate to avoid or reduce expenses. By moving to an area closer to your workplace, you can save on transportation costs and move that money into your savings account. Renting or sharing a home also saves on utilities and maintenance expenses.

Negotiate Bills And Expenses

Don't be afraid to scrutinize your bills for any added expenses that seem unnecessary and might be subject to negotiation. You can always contact your service providers and negotiate cheaper alternative plans, discounts, or promotions. Remember, there is no shame in doing this. You are inquiring about a service with a provider where you are concerned about the service and your payments. As such, you are allowed to ask questions, and they are required to answer them. And no, you won't bother anybody when you ask these questions.

Thrifting

Thrift shops, second-hand stores, and DIYs are gold mines.

Spend some time in a thrift store and make thrifting a fun adventure for the family. Create a list of items you need or want and send them on a treasure hunt. See if the store has what you need or if they have the materials to make it yourself. I have seen people make tables with an old tire and some rope or repurpose a tired, old dresser. Let your imagination run wild! Check out Pinterest or other internet sites for ideas if you're like me and not quite as creative as others. If you think you don't have a creative mind, don't let that hold you back. YouTube is a great place to find videos and get ideas for things you can make for your house. Follow the steps in the video, and voilà! There you have it! Who knows? You might get the hang of it and start making your own how-to videos as a side hustle.

Prioritize Needs Over Wants

Understand the difference between needs and wants. Always take care of necessities like housing and food before purchasing things you want but don't necessarily need. You don't need a new purse if your current one is still functional, and although your kids feel like they will die if they don't have the latest video game or hot toy, I promise they will come out unscathed.

Pause before purchasing to ask if it must be purchased at that very moment or if it's an impulse buy and can be postponed. Avoid shopping on impulse because once you start, it can be challenging to stop (Goldberg, 2024).

Focus on these options to discover what will work best for you. This savings habit will help you sock away money in your savings account while ensuring a steady incoming flow of money. You will be surprised how these small steps can significantly impact the future.

Utilize Windfalls And Bonuses

It may seem too good to be true, but there are moments when you'll receive windfalls, such as tax refunds or bonuses, that will give you a little mental and financial boost. Having these lump sums fall into your lap will make filling up those financial reserves easier.

The key to making the most of these windfalls is to consider them a boost in your savings and allocate a good portion, if not all, to your savings account. Look at it this way, the more stuffing you fit in your savings cushion, the softer your landing will be when life decides to play a prank and throw an unforeseen situation your way. You do remember that furnace going out, don't you?

Suppose you are still busy paying off debts. Windfalls can help speed up debt repayment, which is a big priority in maintaining your financial health, especially post-divorce. Repaying those pesky debts will help ease your mind and remove the weight and worry from your shoulders.

Post-divorce life is a difficult and strange change. You have to move your things around, potentially change your lifestyle, watch and care for the kids, and take care of yourself. It isn't easy to adjust so quickly without panicking about the future. Adding windfalls to your savings helps put your mind at ease that no matter what happens, you have money to rely on in times of need.

I understand windfalls may compel you to splurge on something you really want. I get it; trust me, I do! If you believe using a bit of the amount would motivate you, contribute 50-75% of the windfall money to savings and use the rest to have that splurge you've been craving.

Investing for Growth

After securing your income, making a budget that will cover your necessities, and establishing savings to cover emergencies, you want to grow your wealth by investing your savings. People may fear the risk of putting their money into different investments and decide to forgo this process altogether, but in doing so, they sacrifice growing their savings and wealth.

To invest:

1. Build an agenda for your investments.
2. In it, dedicate one portion of your income to your daily expenses and debt repayment plan.
3. Use another portion to invest in a diverse portfolio and contribute to income growth through potentially higher returns.

If you have no background or investing expertise, obtain help from a professional financial advisor. Financial advisors are trained to examine your financial goals, income, and living situation and create a plan unique to your needs. Their expertise will make the process much easier and much, much safer. Take the time to interview multiple planners and choose the one that fits your financial plan and personality best. If you are a conservative investor, using a planner that invests in higher-risk commodities is definitely not where you want to be.

Handling finances and investments, savings, or constructing financial plans is difficult. It's normal for you to struggle to understand some issues; it can be challenging and time-consuming. A financial planner's expertise lies in this sort of thing, so you can depend on them to understand your point of view when determining a plan to best help you with your situation and future goals.

Make sure your financial planner understands your problems and concerns.

Come clean and be completely honest. They can help with things such as:

- budgeting
- debt management
- investment planning
- retirement planning

Professional finance advisors with experience in divorce financial planning or certified divorce financial analysts (CDFA) are good options to rely on (Thorp, 2021). They will understand your situation and will be able to create strategies and plans for you to follow.

One of the best parts of investing is outpacing inflation and the rising cost of living by preserving your savings and its value. Investing in a diverse portfolio of assets with your financial planner's help will reduce the risk that your investment might drop in a fluctuating market. It helps if you also remain consistent in your investments to promote growth. Having a small portion of your monthly income automatically transferred to your investments is an excellent way to adopt this habit.

Suppose you want an option other than working with a financial planner. In that case, you can find financial help and advice in your local community through non-profit entities, government agencies, and community organizations that provide counseling, workshops, or services. You might be surprised at what you find in your community. Try looking into services provided by local agencies and see if they will work for you.

You can also look into online forums that provide information, tips, tools, plans, and strategies for budgeting, saving, and investing. This information can be found on websites, blogs, articles, etc.

Celebrating Savings Milestones

When you view savings as a game, every goal reached is like scoring another goal. It makes you try harder and strive more to experience that exhilarating feeling of having won. You will feel more in control of your life and be grateful for the support that got you to where you are today. Remain steadfast and strong.

Remember when you were a kid, excitedly waiting as your piggy bank got heavier and heavier until you broke it open to see how much you'd saved. Those days ended with buying something you had been working and saving for.

Although you won't be breaking any piggy banks in the near future, the sentiment remains, making the scrimping and saving along your journey worth it.

Every day, tell yourself, "I'm one step closer to..." and finish the statement with whatever goal you've set for the future. Not only will you live your life and find fun and beauty in the simplest of things in the present, but this will also allow you to peer into the future, where you'll see hope and ambition.

You can also preach this positive mindset to your kids so they can experience the joy of this milestone along with you. Saving may seem tedious, but not if you make it fun!

Let's sum it up …

In this chapter, we've studied the complexities of saving money. Understanding how to set goals, set money aside for savings, discover different ways to save money, and value the milestones you've achieved have all been part of the learning curve.

It's important to value these lessons and this information to apply it effectively in the future. If this seems complicated, take a deep breath and know you aren't alone. Everyone has their own pace and savings plan. Follow through with your savings plan with confidence, drive, and ambition.

No one can stop you from reaching your goals but yourself, and frankly, that's not something you want to do. Open that savings account. Hire a financial planner. Educate yourself on investment portfolios. It is time for you to take action!

Chapter Exercises and Reflections

Here are a few exercises you can do to prioritize saving money while staying motivated.

Analyze Transactions

Review your recent transactions and highlight the things you perceive to be of value, things that help you feel good, things you don't particularly feel anything about, and things you regret purchasing.

This practice will help you identify which purchases are necessities and which represent unnecessary spending that you can cut out the next time and save money.

Practice Discipline

Develop the habit of pausing and assessing your needs before purchasing a product. This habit will help create discipline, and if you prioritize needs over wants, you are less likely to splurge after receiving a bonus.

Set Visual Cues

Visual reminders keep you motivated about your spending habits and goals and can significantly change your lifestyle. Keep these reminders in places you frequent the most in your house and at eye level so they don't go unnoticed. These reminders will condition your mind to remain consistent with your savings and incentivize you to continue your plan.

No-Spend Week Or Month

Challenge yourself to go a day without spending money on anything other than your necessities, such as rent, utilities, bills, and groceries. See how you fare, then make this challenge a bit tougher by increasing the number of no-spend days until you have gone a week without spending. To really up the challenge stakes, increase the number of weeks until you have gone a month without spending.

Take note of your progress, and assess how often you can accomplish this challenge and how long you can maintain it. Can you do a week without spending? A month? Two months out of the year? It all depends on how much discipline you possess. The best way to approach this is to treat it as a challenge and set a limit, only to surpass it and create a new one (Roberge, 2020).

Set Up A Savings Jar

Start a savings jar, store it on the kitchen counter, and put in whatever spare change you have at the end of the day. Have the kids join in and watch as the jar slowly fills with money. How great would it feel to splurge on a fun day or special meal with the kids using money they helped save?

We've discussed several things that can help you save money and motivate you to maintain the savings practice. The key is finding the best methods that suit you and your family. Try looking online or talking to people who have faced similar situations. They may have some helpful advice and tips to share beyond the ones in this book.

A few questions you might ask yourself throughout this process are

- *"What goals do I hope to achieve in the future?"*
- *"How much do I need to save to achieve these goals?"*
- *"What are my savings and budgeting strategies?"*
- *"Do I need professional help to come up with a strategy?"*
- *"What habits and things can I let go of to save money?"*
- *"What local alternatives can I find for the products I consume?"*
- *"Is this item a need or a want?"*
- *"How much of my savings should go into my emergency fund?"*
- *"Should I move to a rental apartment to save money?"*
- *"What do my kids need right now?"*
- *"Does my budget plan need adjusting?"*
- *"How far have I come?"*
- *"Am I satisfied with where my finances are?"*

Keep the answers to these questions in mind as you move forward. It won't be long before looking for a way out of your financial trouble is a thing of the past. No more will you be searching for solutions in the dark. Every question you ask yourself and every answer you're able to give will shed a bit of light. This is when you'll notice all the different directions you can take toward achieving your goals, and you'll be able to figure out the best ones based on your strengths.

Stay strong and move forward.

Chapter 9:

Credit Comeback: Navigating the Impact of Divorce on Your Credit Score and Building a Financially Empowered Future

"Sorting through all the debts after my first divorce was depressing, to say the least. Even taking into account that my husband took on half the debts per our divorce agreement, I knew I was in way over my head with a reduced income and two small children. I made my budgets, negotiated the debt as much as possible, cut expenses, and did all I could to figure out how to get out of the hole I found myself in. I tried credit counseling sites and spent a ton of time researching all my options. It didn't take long to realize the only option I had at the time to salvage any bit of my credit was to sacrifice my pride and dignity and file for bankruptcy. Filing was among the most humbling and embarrassing things I've ever done. I was raised a farmer's daughter and was taught always to pay my debts. But I gathered all my loan and credit card statements, made lists of all my assets, and met with a bankruptcy attorney. I remember the biggest frustration in filing was that I gathered all the paperwork, paid all the fees (including the attorney), went through all the humiliation, and my ex benefited from it all when all the accounts included in my bankruptcy also relieved him from paying his half of all the debts-without it costing

him a dime. But today, my credit score is "excellent," I'm never worried about applying for a mortgage or vehicle loan, and my investment portfolio is growing daily. "

In the after-divorce frenzy, it's easy to use credit cards to pay for all the expenses you never knew you would have to contend with. But when there's finally a pause in your traumatized financial life, the first creditor is right outside your doors or on the phone, demanding the money back and threatening you with bad credit if you fail to pay.

What are you supposed to do in such a situation?

You might remember an adult in your childhood telling you, "Money doesn't grow on trees." Ah, the good old days when money did seem like it grew on trees and you didn't have a financial care in the world. Unfortunately, your bubble has been cruelly burst, and now you know what those adults meant.

What do you do when you're out of money, can't borrow anymore, and can't afford to return what you've already borrowed?

Oh, how we wish money grew on trees.

When you come face-to-face with your post-divorce credit score, some of those old financial insecurities may rise again:

- *"Will my divorce always be a black stain on my credit score?"*
- *"Why should a divorce even affect my credit score?"*
- *"It wasn't just my fault! Why does the whole world and even the BANK care about my divorce, for goodness sake!"*
- *"Everyone's turned against me. Even my credit card limits have decreased!"*
- *"Will I ever have decent credit again?!"*

According to the Legal and General website, women generally see their incomes fall about 33.33% after divorce ("Divorce Gap," 2021). Add to that any legal fees and joint debts, and it's easy to quickly max out the credit card while navigating the first few months of your divorce just trying to keep your head above water. Then, add insult to injury when you don't have the funds to pay on your credit cards and loans and miss a few payments.

Does this sound familiar? If it does, your credit score probably took a hit because you needed money at that low point in your life, and you did what had to be done to pay the rent, keep the lights on, and feed the kids. It had nothing to do with the divorce itself.

It's essential to keep an eye on your credit score because fixing your credit score after the fact will take some time and may impact your borrowing ability in the future.

What Is A Credit Score?

So, what does a credit report do? It tells lenders about your credit accounts and how you've managed your credit. Every time you apply to borrow money, creditors check this report. A credit score predicts your ability to repay a loan based on your credit history factors such as the number of debt accounts you have open, the total amount of outstanding debt, your repayment history, etc. Lenders use a three-digit number, usually between 300 and 850, to assess whether they are willing to lend you money and how much interest they will charge you.

Assessing Your Current Credit Situation

As we discussed, a divorce can impact your credit by drastically decreasing your income and repayment ability, or you may have gone into a spiral of desperate spending and spotty repayment before you could gather your emotions and find a stable job. Your joint accounts and shared debts divided in your divorce can also impact your score with high balances or missed payments when you were married. Credit inaccuracies could also affect your credit score.

You are entitled to a free annual credit report from each of the three USA credit reporting agencies. Log in to the three consumer reporting bureaus (Equifax, Experian, and TransUnion) to check your credit report and score (they're separate things, so be sure to ask for both). Get credit reports from all three bureaus to cross-check for inaccuracies, and be aware credit scores will differ slightly from one company to the next because they calculate it differently, but it's best to know everything you can ("Free," n.d.; "5 Ways to Improve," 2023).

Contrary to popular opinion, checking your credit report won't harm your credit score; it's only when lenders check it that the report might be affected by a credit inquiry. Keeping that in mind, don’t ask a third party, such as a bank or other financial institution, to check your credit reports, as that may negatively impact your credit score.

You can also keep tabs on your report via apps like CreditKarma.com or CreditSesame.com without affecting your score. Although they may not be as accurate as an official agency score, they help you keep up with any adverse reporting that may go terribly sideways if you don't catch it for an entire year. Another cool thing is you can check your score monthly (or more often if you wish) via these apps to watch your score increase rather than waiting twelve months for that ego boost.

Look carefully at your credit reports and constantly check them for accuracy. Ensure you are removed from any cards your spouse is accountable for per your divorce decree so the repayment history or credit balance doesn't show up on your report. Also, close or remove your spouse from any joint cards the courts said you are responsible for repaying so your spouse can't continue to increase balances on that debt. Be vigilant and figure out what caused your credit score to change so you can take steps to remedy the situation.

Addressing Joint Debts

Since your credit score is this all-important number that defines who will lend you money, you need to ensure that you control everything about your credit and that your ex's transactions won't affect you. Here's where to start planning your actions.

Your joint debt may be **secured, unsecured,** or **authorized**. Let's unpack these as they may pertain to your divorce.

In the case of **secured** debt, the spouse keeping the asset (car, house, or boat, for example) generally has to pay up. So, if your ex is awarded the vehicle you've been paying for together, they will have to pay for the remainder of the loan. However, if they miss payments, get repossessed, or have a foreclosure, it will show up on your credit report because the loan was a joint one. Though this might sound unfair, it can be fixed. Ask your ex (or ask the courts to tell your ex) to refinance the car or house and remove you from all loan responsibility for an asset you no longer possess.

If the debt is **unsecured** but still joint, the divorce court could order each of you to move half of the credit to respective new credit cards or personal loans in your individual names and close the joint account.

In both cases, the credit history for the accounts—even if you close them off and transfer the balance—stays on both accounts' credit histories for ten years before it expires. It is essential to be extremely vigilant and close the accounts immediately to prevent any new purchases by your spouse on your joint accounts.

In the case of an **authorized** account, one spouse "owns" the account and is responsible for paying off the loan. The other spouse was "authorized" to use the account and most likely issued their own card.

While you were married, both spouses shared the responsibility for payment, so the credit history goes on both reports. But when you get divorced, the authorized spouse can remove the unauthorized one from the account which means they can no longer incur any additional debt on the account. In this case, the credit history won't appear on the other spouse's credit report. If you're the account owner, the court can make the authorized spouse pay for half of the balance on these cards incurred during your marriage, even if you took the card out in your name. (Akin, 2023).

The divorce court should help you deal with joint debts, but be sure nothing is left out and that you separate on fair terms. It is equally important to ensure your name is no longer associated with any debts the court has assigned to your spouse. After all, who wants to lose their marriage *and* their credit at the same time?

Dealing with Creditors and Lenders

Here we are, back at negotiations. I know you're sick and tired of the term because of all the hassle, preparation, confidence-boosting, and just plain bravery you need to face a negotiator, but you must take the bull by the horns. You can do this!

Have mercy on "Future You", grit your teeth, and dive into the battle arena. This time, you will inform lenders of your circumstances by telling them that your missed payments are because you're going through a rough patch, but you're still reliable.

Since you've probably changed several things regarding account ownership, credit cards, balances, and the like, you need to note all of these changes. Inform all your lenders about your change in marital status (and if you've changed your name, be sure to get that changed with them also). Be honest and open and assure them that you will continue being responsible for your debt and are determined to repay it.

Creditors want you to pay back the borrowed amount because if you file for bankruptcy, they'll get very little (if anything) out of the deal. Keep this in mind as you negotiate. After assuring the lender that you're serious about paying back the money you owe, ask them for some leniency in the payment plan or some other way to settle the balance faster. The negotiator might be okay with taking less money than you owe them. In some cases, you may be able to settle for

50% of the amount you owe them. However you negotiate, keep some concession for your credit score as part of the deal.

Here are some tips to help you through the negotiation process. It's not much different from the talks we went through for debt settlement in Chapter 5. The gist is to begin by offering a lump sum of money—since you're settling your accounts anyway, why not try to start over by closing everything related to your past? Start by offering a lump sum of 30% of the amount owed. The lender might be okay with accepting the lump sum payment offer and letting you go before it's too late for them to get anything at all. The only catch to this strategy is having the cash on hand to pay them.

Alternatively, negotiate to pay a reduced amount of the total you owe spread out in monthly payments. (Try offering 50% of the total to begin with.) You must negotiate a comfortable monthly payment plan for the amount you'll pay. A payment concession that only leads to drowning in interest and monthly payments again completely defeats the purpose of negotiating.

Negotiate hard because you already know how difficult it is to make ends meet after a divorce. Your goal is to get some break from creditors. Relief from high loan payments will be worth the hassle of negotiating.

Rebuilding Credit After Divorce

They say that showing up is often one of the hardest parts of the battle.

You must know *why* you're doing something with utmost conviction so you won't lose your motivation halfway through the journey. Return to your notebook where you wrote down your Big Dream and your "why" for gaining financial independence. Review your long-term goals to remind yourself why you are putting in all this effort to raise your credit score.

Your answer will be personal, but I'll help. It's because you want to get more credit in the future and at lower interest rates. Good credit means you'll likely be able to borrow more. Emotionally, good credit should give you peace of mind because you're on top of your minimum payments and any critical debt-related issues, and that's more than what many people can say. Intellectually and emotionally, fixing your credit score is in your favor. Make debt repayment a priority both logically and for your emotional well-being.

Now that you realize the importance of fixing your credit score let's review some things that can affect it.

- When you apply for a loan, the lender will check your credit history. This check results in a "hard inquiry," and an excessive number of hard inquiries can impact your credit score for up to two years.
- Missed or late payments look bad because they suggest you may not repay the loan and could default.
- You use most of the credit available to you. The more money you borrow, the greater your likelihood of getting in trouble. Your credit utilization rate will tell you how much of your available credit you have used up. Using more than 30% of your available credit will lower your credit score.
- The age of your credit accounts will also affect your score. Opening new credit card accounts will disproportionately increase your available credit and make the lender nervous that you may get in over your head with credit card debt. On the other hand, don't close an old credit card account, as this reduces your available credit ("Is It Okay," 2023).

At the very least, if you can't make additional payments on your cards to relieve your debt load, focus on minimum payments. Suppose everything goes upside down in your financial life, but you make all your minimum payments. In that case, your lenders will have nothing to complain about as you are paying them the agreed amounts, and they will report your accounts to the credit agencies as in good standing. Your credit history will improve as you make timely monthly payments.

With minimum payments under control, you can now work on reducing your outstanding debt as per the **debt repayment plan** you set up earlier. Motivate yourself by thinking about the debt-free life you'll be living if you're consistent with getting rid of your debt. There's no better feeling of freedom than knowing you don't owe money to anyone.

Two things happen as you start getting rid of debt and improving your payment history. First, your credit card companies might increase your credit limit. Increasing your credit limit can improve your credit score because your credit utilization ratio decreases. Second, with your new credit score, you can get a new loan with a lower interest rate to refinance your high-interest credit cards. See the catch-22 work in your favor? It's amazing!

For example (with arbitrary amounts), say you owe $6000 for a credit card, and your credit limit is $16,000. You've taken out more than 30% of your available credit.

You pay off $1,000, but your credit limit stays at $16,000. You now owe $5,000 but are still using more than 30% of your available credit.

Your credit score has increased because of your excellent track record of timely payments. The bank is happy with your credit score and has increased your limit to $16,750. Now, you're only using 29.8% of your available credit even though you haven't paid any extra to get there.

See what I mean?

Since you want to wean yourself off the credit card, you can draw on your improved credit score to find a lender who will refinance your debt into one loan with a lower interest rate. You'll win all around! Let the thought of this win and expediting the process of becoming debt-free motivate you along your journey.

Establishing Credit for Beginners

This chapter might sound like gibberish to some of you (perhaps lucky) readers because you have yet to have a credit card. At many points, you might have felt elated that you're not deep in credit card debt because of how difficult it sounds (and is) to get out of.

However, it is a good idea to establish a credit score. With a credit score, you can easily get loans for things like a house, car, or similarly expensive asset.

The first way to do this—and perhaps the easiest—is to become an **authorized user** on a trusted friend or family member's card. This way, you can share their credit history, as their credit will also appear on your report for that card. You don't need to make any purchases to benefit as an authorized user on the card history when building a credit score.

Choose the friend or family member wisely because any lousy credit on their card will also appear on your report. It's a fair trade as long as you're both responsible. On the fun side, you'll also benefit from any perks associated with the credit card, like airport lounge access.

Another avenue is to get a secured credit card. A secured card is issued when you deposit some money, and that amount becomes your credit limit. You'll be charged interest if you borrow against that amount for an extended period. On the flip side, you can also earn rewards. These cards are easier to qualify for, and once you have earned a good credit history, you can switch to an unsecured card.

Third, you can build a score without having a credit card if you pay for your cell phone, utilities, and certain streaming service bills through your bank account with a tool like Experian Boost. These tools track your payments, document your on-time payments, and use them to add to your credit score.

Always be diligent about your credit utilization rates (never use more than 30% of your available credit) and payment history. Pay ahead, and make small transactions on groceries and everyday items as you build your credit. If you pay these off quickly, you'll incur minimal interest, if any. You can keep your credit score momentum going, even on a tight budget.

These factors are, first and foremost, contributors to your credit score. Keep things in check, and you'll start building your credit history within two to six months.

The bottom line is that a good credit score comes in handy when you need a large loan with a reasonable interest rate. Luckily, it's easy to build credit without getting a credit card or paying excessive interest (Wilder & White, 2024).

Creating a Credit Repair Plan

You have your options; now lay them out as you've practiced with budgeting, debt repayment, contingency, earning, etc., and devise a credit repair plan.

Choose the options that suit you best and add in the pieces of credit you can negotiate. Next, determine the steps, deadlines, sub-steps, and anything that will get you to the action stage and write them in your plan.

Prepare and motivate yourself by setting a clear strategy that you can accomplish reasonably without losing hope in its difficulty and without underestimating your potential. Your credit repair plan must suit your work ethic and priorities for it to work.

Work out how you will:

- assess your debt using your credit report and credit score

- separate your accounts from your ex's (if there are any still left)
- negotiate with your creditors to see if there's any leeway
- rebuild your credit if you don't have a robust credit history
- maintain healthy credit habits by meeting payments and reducing the use of credit cards
- factor in budgeting
- access credit counseling (If you need it)

Once again, incorporate this plan into your overall financial goals so everything will be in one place.

Developing Healthy Credit Habits

We've touched upon this in more detail before, but allow me to repeat it because I can't stress this enough: you *have* to continue with healthy credit management if you are to stay stable in the long term. There will come a time when you'll be able to spend freely out of your earnings but now is not the time. It isn't enough to keep your head above the water. If you want to swim and eventually get to shore, you must put in constant, rigorous effort.

So, I reiterate: **maintain a good payment history**. You should never fall short of your minimum payments. If you have that under control, reduce the amount of credit you're using. You need to work to reduce the borrowed amount to zero.

If you don't have a credit history, start to build one without accumulating debt. Do it solely for the future, when you might need an immediate, short-term loan for a lucrative investment or want to purchase a house. Even then, prioritize investing your savings over taking out loans.

While working on credit management, you must keep your debt management goals in view. This means constant vigilance against the dark forces of debt.

To stay consistent with debt reduction—the key to good credit—you must start seeing debt as a villain who can't wait to squeeze the lifeblood out of you. Think of Hansel and Gretel, who couldn't resist the witch's sweets and walked right into her trap out of their own free will. Were they to blame? They were hungry, but as an adult who knows exactly who lives inside that sweet-clad house, do you think you should venture inside? I don't think so.

Once more, draw on your childhood; only this time, resist the sweet temptation of the credit card that promises you all you want in exchange for the witch inside, who will drain your resources, one interest cycle at a time.

Budgeting for Credit Health

By now, you should have your credit history and habits sorted, but I want to remind you that your budget—which you've already (hopefully) created—plays an integral role in your credit health. When you have money from your earnings in your hand and make the minimum payments, pay the bills, and cover the necessities of life, it's incredibly tempting to treat yourself. Many around you are still in debt precisely because they can't resist the urge to gratify themselves, spending everything they earn instantly. Don't settle for that. You've worked too hard on your financial journey.

It is said that the circumstances of your birth are out of your control, but you can work toward the circumstances of your situation for when you die. Where you are now might be because of your divorce, but where you choose to be ten years down the road is, as you just read, a choice. Make it wisely.

If you live hand-to-mouth now, with little to spare, set aside just a little to reduce your debt. Little by little, drop by drop, pay off your debts and reduce the interest you're accumulating. Reduce your standard of living to the bare minimum with the promise that you'll move on to something much better than you've ever had if you keep at it. Prioritize the money drain, which is debt and interest, and you'll be surprised at how the debt reduction clears out and amplifies your spending power. You need to look beyond the euphoria of the seemingly infinite buying power the credit card gives you in the short term before it cripples you.

Seeking Professional Credit Counseling

I've constantly maintained that counseling is nothing to be ashamed of. If you need help figuring out this world between the realms of cold, hard cash and the confusion of credit, it's totally reasonable! You are dealing with the distinctly human emotions of grief, separation, and helplessness after your divorce, especially if your kids need you to be strong, and it's okay to look for help to understand your financial situation and all the options.

Debt is an overwhelming burden you might not know how to handle, and it's okay to seek out specialized credit counseling services from a professional who has guided many other women out of a fix like yours. You are not alone—everyone has lows and weaknesses.

However, when you're looking for counseling, look for a firm that isn't going to add to your debt by being a money-making scheme itself. Stay aware of a trap where the company claims to be a nonprofit or certified. Take the time to thoroughly research anyone claiming to help you out of a financial hardship.

One agency I suggest is American Consumer Credit Counseling (ACCC), which offers the first session for free and a debt management plan for $50 ("Reputable," 2021). They offer help with debt management and bankruptcy counseling and have vast resources for everything from budgeting to college planning. You can reach them at https://www.consumercredit.com/.

Whatever agency you choose, make sure it has good reviews, experience, and affordability. If it is an option, try a free session before committing to a program.

Building Positive Financial Relationships

As you move on with your life, you will meet new people and start new relationships. Always think about your relationship in terms of how you will manage finances. While you were married, you may have taken the back seat and let your partner handle the money matters; this is one reason you're having difficulty learning about finances now. Next time, however, you're better prepared because you know how money works.

If you choose to begin a new relationship, think about building a healthy relationship with money, as well. As a team, you can collaborate to manage your credit, avoiding the pitfalls that gave you trouble the last time. By pooling your resources and having two income streams for the household, you can work on budgeting for more room for debt repayment and savings.

You will invest together in your future while ensuring your joint goals match. By pooling your interests, you will become partners in making the finances work, eliminating debt, and maximizing your investments. That way, even in an emergency, you won't have to draw on credit and will begin your new relationship on the right financial track.

Monitoring and Protecting Your Credit

While you work your way out of debt, it is essential to ensure that no one will take advantage of your hard work. Hacking and identity theft enable people to impersonate someone and use their credit to make purchases easily, so you need to be aware of how you share your personal information.

Earlier in this chapter, I mentioned inaccuracies in your credit report. Sometimes, you might see unfamiliar activity on your credit report. A new loan or credit card has been opened that you didn't initiate. A purchase for a new refrigerator shows up on your credit card, but you didn't purchase one. These could be signs that your account has been compromised. You need to be vigilant and be on the lookout for such instances. Check your credit report frequently and your credit card statement even more often.

If you believe your account has been compromised, the first thing to do is to set up a **fraud alert**. Ask lenders to verify your identity before issuing credit in your name. Second, set a **credit** or **security freeze** so no one can access your account until you "thaw" it. For this, you must email "the three national credit bureaus to limit access to your credit reports indefinitely" (Akin, 2023a). A credit freeze blocks legitimate checks and requests until you thaw the account after dealing with the unfamiliar activity. A fraud alert adds a new layer of security in which the lender must confirm it's you before approving transactions. It expires after some time and must be renewed.

Here are some things to remember that will protect your information in the first place.

- Don't store credit card information at e-commerce sites; it's convenient but risky.
- Create strong, unique passwords for all accounts and change them often.
- Use two-factor authentication where possible,
- Don't shop online using public Wi-Fi accounts.
- Protect your personal information, login credentials, and other information in places where someone can't hear or see it (Akin, 2023a).

Celebrating Credit Milestones

Congratulations! If you've made it this far, you're well on your way to battling your debt. As a final step, every time you complete one of your credit repair goals, you should allow yourself some room to celebrate. Every time you check your credit report and score to find that it has gone up significantly, every time your credit limit increases on an account, and every time you fall below 30% of the credit utilization on a card is all evidence of how far you've come, from relying on your credit to minimizing your use of it, and then moving toward positive credit.

Everyone who has been where you are or who is struggling along with you should be so proud of what you're doing—way to go!

Here's a quick overview to sum up all you've learned about credit.

Begin by assessing your credit, ensuring there is no leftover joint credit from your marriage. Get credit reports and scores and negotiate payment plans with lenders. Rebuild good credit with a credit repair plan, using budgeting techniques, vigilance, and counseling to teach good credit-related habits. Finally, celebrate your milestones as you begin acting on your plan.

Spare a few moments to reflect upon your journey from being in debt to repairing your credit. It's a long and challenging path, but think about how you'll feel at the end of this tedious process. It will stop being tedious if you enjoy learning new things. Just imagine—when we started, you didn't know how to manage a credit card properly, and here you are, independently handling financial negotiations as you find your way through life. Isn't the feeling intoxicating?

A famous quote attributed to historical hero Titu Mir (n.d.) goes, "To live like a lion for a day is far better than to live for a hundred years like a jackal." Learning to live like a lion—free and in control of your life—is a worthy endeavor, undoubtedly worth all the effort you've put into your learning curve.

Chapter Exercises and Reflections

By now, you should be able to discern a pattern in your finances.

First, you assess. Ask,

- *"What is the problem?"*
- *"Why is it a problem?"*
- *"What's the extent of the problem?"*

Then, look at how to fix the problem because divorces happen, and there are ways to deal with whatever you're going through.

Then ask,

- *"Okay, so I'm in a mess—what are my options? What are the pros and cons of each option?"*

Third, you plan. Use the SMART goal-setting method we learned and ask,

- *"So, I've got my options sorted—which option should I take? What are the steps? How long will each step take?"*
- *"Do I need counseling to help me decide between the options?"*

Fourth, you act. This is where all the negotiations, saving, debt-reducing and earning strategies, credit building, and actions from your planning stages come into the real world.

- *"What's the next step on the list?"*
- *"Was the last step successful?"*
- *If not, "What do I do next?"*

Fifth, you celebrate! Acknowledge your progress at significant milestones to motivate yourself to continue to the next step of your planning process. Tell yourself, *"Yay! We made it!"*

Repeat the loop from assessing to celebrating as many times as you need, and keep acting as you figure things out on the fly. You know the basics; now it's time to master them by putting them into practice.

Let's look at how this might play out with your questions about credit management. First, assess:

- *"What is the problem with my credit score?"*
- *"Why is my credit history becoming a problem?"*
- *"What's the extent of my credit mismanagement?"*

Next, remind yourself that you have options.

If they're related to assessing credit, tell yourself that you can go for counseling or DIY.

If you're new to credit cards, "To establish credit, I can either piggyback on my friend or take a secured loan, which can get risky."

To repair your credit, tell yourself that either you can negotiate with your creditors and do the math for your credit repair plan or pay a counselor to do it for you.

If you fear you might be a victim of fraud, tell yourself that you can freeze your account or set up a fraud alert in an emergency.

For all options, ask yourself:

- *"Which option should I take? What are the steps I should take? What are the pros and cons? How long will each step take?"*
- *"Do I need counseling to help me decide?"*

Next, as you act, keep asking:

- *"What's the next step on the list?"*
- *"Was the last step successful?"*

After every step, leave room to congratulate yourself for coming this far

Feel free to reflect, take a long walk or meditate for your mental health—whatever helps you think—as you ask yourself the questions above, and let your answers guide your actions.

Chapter 10:

Thriving After Divorce: Celebrating Independence and Charting a Bold Future Reflecting on the Journey

Upon reaching the final chapter of this book, take the opportunity to look back to see how far you've come. It seems surreal. Hopefully, this financial journey has been liberating from the start to the end.

Think back to the beginning of your journey, how scary everything seemed to be, and how the word 'divorce' left a horrible taste in your mouth. By reading this book, you've learned all about life's ups and downs and the dos and don'ts of your finances after divorce. You're now fully equipped to take on the world as a financially independent woman.

Celebrate every little milestone, no matter how small. You deserve it! Every step you've taken has brought you closer to living an independent life. Your identity is yours to dictate; it's no longer there to share with your partner. It is up to you to forge a financial identity you'll be proud of and can take with you as you build new relationships. You can transform yourself into a whole new being, someone you've always dreamed of being, or stay true to the qualities you already have but strut with a bit more confidence; the choice is up to you.

Know that you are fabulous for gathering the courage and determination to go through the divorce process with confidence and control. Now that you're prepared to be independent, the surge of power you feel must be incredible to experience. However, remember the support you've had along the way from family, friends, and professionals. You don't have to face your journey alone.

Celebrating Personal Achievements

Divorce is a stressful process. It takes your emotions on an amusement ride through hell, and it's even worse for the wear and tear it inflicts on the mind. No one expects you to remain stoic, firm, or confident 100% of the time, but look at where you're standing now.

Have you achieved what you desired?

If there were things you've been fighting for, did you win the fight?

No matter the case, you've emerged on the other side of divorce with strength and resilience. Honestly, it's challenging to reach out to others for help and talk about our lives, whether with loved ones or professionals. I remember it felt like I was putting the entirety of my life on display for them to judge, and I'd wait for the "You're so stupid!" or "I told you so" comments.

It's terrifying, but look at you now. You're on the path of freedom from those God-awful emotions that kept you feeling as if you were ruining the lives of everyone around you. Yes, the memories of the life that once was may come back to haunt you. Those memories might be full of happiness, sorrow, or melancholy, but divorce doesn't mean you must entirely forget that part of your life. They can simply be memories you learn from so you can move forward in life with a better understanding of yourself, a greater expectation of the world, and a new approach to navigating through life.

This newfound freedom can also be an opportunity for you to reach out and share your story with others who have faced or are facing similar situations.

It is time for you to look forward to your life as an independent woman and set new goals for the future. These can be as small as discovering a new hobby or as big as starting another relationship. The choice is yours.

Navigating Emotional Healing

Facing a myriad of emotions is also a part of moving on. You might think things like,

- *"I'm happy I'm finally free from the situation, so why am I crying?"*
- *"I know I can't do anything now, but I am so angry I could scream!"*

The aftermath of divorce comes with many emotions, both positive and negative. There is no correct way of going about them because everyone's experience and situation differ. We all do the best we can. However, try not to push these feelings away to look strong. No one expects you to be on point one hundred percent of the time. It's okay to take time to grieve. Actually, it's super important you take that time.

If you push your feelings away, they'll accumulate until they blow up in a massive breakdown. Allow yourself to feel your emotions, and try to understand why you feel them. When you process these emotions, they will start to settle the raging storm in your mind, and it will all become a bad memory.

Next, know your boundaries. What boundaries still exist, and what new ones do you want to establish? Decide on what you are and aren't comfortable with in future friendships and relationships. Understand that you are healing, and be compassionate about your healing process. Don't get angry at yourself for not getting better "fast enough" when that is not how you would react to others having the same experience. You deserve that love as well. You will heal faster if your mind and body believe they are loved.

Achieving Financial Independence

We have discussed multiple strategies, budgeting tricks, and ways to keep yourself afloat so you can become financially independent. When you feel stuck, and it seems as if all is lost, try revisiting the pages of this book to find your way out again. From emergency funds to long-term goals, you discovered many things you had no idea you had to think about. With this knowledge, you can look forward to a successful future.

You no longer have to fear or run from the shadow of debt when you have the information and means to drive it away. Dealing with your fear may seem difficult initially, but with a single step in the right direction, you have begun to mark your way to financial freedom.

Embracing Independence

Your possibilities are endless. Your new financial freedom will allow you to be self-reliant and make decisions that are good for your future goals while being fiscally aware.

It's time to step out of your comfort zone and realize the autonomy you hold in your life. Think carefully about the decisions you need to make and how they'll affect you as you make them. This is why so many strategies are offered in this book, so you can choose the one that best fits your situation.

I've already mentioned how you can rediscover your identity, practice self-care, and recreate boundaries for future relationships. At the same time, you need to understand that you'll be walking through life independently. This independence may be daunting for some, as you make decisions for your family without the second opinion or support system you have become accustomed to. Take a moment to return to the steps outlined here, take a deep breath, and make the decision. Whether it is the right or wrong decision, YOU made it with all the knowledge you have accumulated.

You are responsible for controlling how your life leads. Take the reins with confidence and determination to face the future head-on.

Crafting a Vision For The Future

When you approach life as independent, you can't "wing it." You must consider multiple responsibilities, such as debt repayment, lifestyle, necessities, and kids.

That's where meticulous planning comes in. Imagine yourself in a few months or years—what do you hope to accomplish by then? What should be your short- and long-term goals?

Understand that things won't always remain the same, and your life constantly changes. Accept that change is a part of growth, and take control by visualizing and planning. You must rely on yourself to survive in the world. Become someone you can depend on. That can only come with gaining self-confidence and building an action plan.

You will get through this. You're allowed to make mistakes; everyone does, so don't put yourself down for making them. Tell yourself it's okay, and plan to bounce back. You are capable and powerful; you just need to tap into that.

Fostering a Positive Mindset

It's interesting how an optimistic mind and attitude can play essential roles in physical health. I've mentioned the mind-body connection before and how having a positive mindset allows the body to work well.

If you want an independent future, develop a positive mindset. Wallowing in past regrets will not do you any good; the only thing this accomplishes is trapping yourself in time. Look toward the future and the outside world through a new lens. There is much to discover as an independent individual and many new things to experience.

Know that this book is always an arm's length away and will always be there, so you won't ever freak out about the unknown. Take every day one step at a time, and find happiness in the little things, even the most simple ones.

Set morning and night routines for yourself to maintain a state of normalcy, but don't stop yourself from venturing outside the box to seek new experiences. Always stay curious about the world around you. Surround yourself with optimistic people, and laugh with your whole heart to truly enjoy life as it was meant to be.

It's also important to remember that words have power, so avoid using negative self-talk and show yourself some compassion with positive affirmations. Your mind will begin to believe them, and you'll feel healthier. Love yourself because you deserve to be loved as much as you love others ("Don't Worry," 2022).

Celebrating Independence Day

Celebrate the day your divorce became official as your personal Independence Day. Look forward to this anniversary every year and have a blast doing the most liberating and enjoyable things on that day.

Want to have a night of drinks with your best buddies? A day of extreme adventure around the city? A day full of self-care? Go ahead because nothing is stopping you from using your leisure savings as you wish. This freedom to make your own budgeting decisions is one of the perks of being financially independent. The possibilities are endless. Open the creative doors of your mind and begin planning to rewrite those awful memories with fun ones.

Gratitude and Acknowledgment

Gratitude and acknowledgment come with keeping a positive mindset. Look back on everything and everyone who has helped you get to where you are now. Be grateful for the help you've received; not everyone has the same opportunities available.

Be grateful for the determination and mental strength that brought you to this book and this moment. You've successfully overcome divorce's turmoil and emotional mess and emerged on the other side.

Continuing the Journey

This is not the end. On the contrary—it's just the beginning. You have a whole independent life to live before you. I'm not saying it won't be scary; it most definitely will be. It won't be a smooth ride, either. The earlier chapters of this book have spoken a lot about the many problems that can come up when navigating the world alone, but as Alfred A. Monapert says, "Expect problems and eat them for breakfast" (Tredgold, 2016).

Hey, if you got this far in life, I know damn well you'll be able to get even further.

Final Words of Empowerment

What more is there to say besides that I believe in you and your capability as a woman to lead a joyful and prosperous life without being financially dependent on others? You can take care of yourself and your family as you see fit. You are capable of enjoying life, experiencing its hardships, and growing from it.

People may talk and have many opinions about how you should live your life; however, it's what you think about yourself and your life and whether you're satisfied with it that matters. If not, you must work hard to attain that satisfaction. If we live according to how other people want to see us, we'll lose more and more of our identities every day.

Face the world with a smile, knowing you have an action plan and a will strong enough to overcome anything.

Chapter Exercise and Reflections

Here are some prompts and exercises you can use to reflect on your past and present and think about the future:

The Practice of Reflection

- What went well today?
- What should I change for tomorrow?
- Given what I learned today, how should I solve this problem if I face it again?
- What should I stop doing to prevent this from ever happening again?

Celebrating Achievements

- What am I proud of?
- What would I like to celebrate?
- What have I accomplished today, big or small?

Learning From Challenges

- How did I overcome the problems I faced last year?
- Did I get help from others? If so, who?
- How did those challenges change me?
- I should celebrate my accomplishment of facing those challenges.

Role of Self-Compassion

- I will be kinder to myself.
- I am my friend.
- I did my best, and I'm proud of myself for trying.
- I know I can do it; I just need to figure out a way.
- Perhaps a breath of fresh air is what I need.
- I'm capable, but I need help sometimes, and that's okay.

Planning for the Year Ahead

- What should I change this year?

- Do I need to adjust my budget for the year?
- Will I be able to afford this trip, or should I save up?
- Do I have any deadlines coming up that might alter my priorities?
- What new places will I discover this year?

These questions and thoughts will give you the room to experience self-reflection and lead a life with intention. It will help you recognize your purpose and aims rather than go through life drifting and lost (Angelone, 2024).

Another way to self-reflect is to write down your thoughts and experiences in a journal and revisit the journal with a clear mind to analyze what has happened. You may learn new techniques for handling specific situations or something about yourself that you want to change. You may also find times when you're proud of yourself as you face a challenge or successfully deal with a debt repayment deadline.

It will allow you to see yourself differently and truly appreciate your abilities and strengths (Neale, 2021).

"I think we should get a divorce."

Those six words that rocked my world, made me doubt myself, and threw me into emotional turmoil have turned out to be the best six words I could have ever hoped to hear. Since then, I have rebuilt my financial life, met and married the love of my life, and stood in my truth. The emotional and financial growth I have experienced due to my divorces has made me the strong, independent woman I am today and pushed me to write and publish this book. I know I can face any situation with courage and self-love. Perhaps I need to thank my ex for his decision because I know now, beyond a shadow of a doubt, that I am fearless in facing the possibilities of my life.

My wish for you, dear reader, is to stand with me in your courage and financial independence.

Conclusion

It's strange to reach the end of a book and still have so many words to say. Life is a peculiar thing that chews you up and spits you out on the most random of occasions, and you're left wondering, "Why me?"

That is what I went through. My story and my experience were challenging, just as yours is right now. The struggle I went through and how I emerged from that struggle made me realize that if I'm capable, other women are, too. But what about those women who are unaware of their power, just as I was?

This book is for those women who are unaware of their capabilities. My experience drove me to write this book, to tell my story in the hope that it'll prevent someone from facing the same things, making their journey shorter so they'll suffer less.

I express myself here as a closing note so that I can reach out a hand to you and let you know that you're not alone. There are other women out there who feel what you feel. The sooner we realize that we are together, the more we grow confident in our abilities.

"If she can do it, why can't I?"

"I'll make my way!"

Shout it out as often as needed; know that the only one stopping you is yourself. Let yourself loose, and watch as you take control of your world.

Good luck!

With Peace and Love,

Tracy

Printed in Great Britain
by Amazon

53325669R00099